Thinking on Paper

Also by V. A. Howard

Artistry: the Work of Artists (1982)

THINKING ON PAPER

V. A. Howard, Ph.D., and J. H. Barton, M.A.

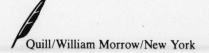
Quill/William Morrow/New York

Library of Congress Cataloging-in-Publication Data

Howard, V.A. (Vernon A.), 1937–
Thinking on paper.

Bibliography: p.
Includes index.
1. English language—Rhetoric. 2. English language—
Grammar—1950–   . I. Barton, J. H.   II Title.
PE1408.H68525   1986   808'.042   86-5270
ISBN 0-688-07758-7 (pbk.)

Printed in the United States of America

First Quill Edition

1 2 3 4 5 6 7 8 9 10

BOOK DESIGN BY VICTORIA HARTMAN

To our teachers and critics
past, present, and future

Acknowledgments

The authors are grateful to all who contributed to the progress of this book. They came from many different walks of life, as befits a book of this kind: scientists, philosophers, educators, journalists, consultants, students, and friends. Of necessity writers all, they took a critical and hearty interest in this project, which pushed us on when we found it difficult to push ourselves. Whatever their different interests and occupations, a common interest in becoming better writers helped to put this little volume into your hands.

To the following we are especially indebted:

Our colleagues at the Philosophy of Education Research Center at Harvard: Professor Katherine Elgin, Dr. Kenneth Hawes, Dr. Norman Katz, Dr. David N. Perkins, and Professor Israel Scheffler, co-director of the center, for their painstaking scrutiny of the text at every stage. Professor Scheffler deserves special mention for his moral support as well as his canny insights into the mind's workings.

The John Dewey Foundation for its support of V. A. Howard's researches on this and other projects having to do with learning and experience. We entertain ourselves with the fiction that, had Dewey written a companion volume to his

How We Think (1933) called *How We Write,* it might have borne some resemblance to the present volume.

James B. Ayres of *The Boston Globe,* Barbara Dewan of Radio Shack, and Paul E. McLaughlin, consultant, whose supportive instruction helped relieve the authors of their ingrained fear of computers.

Maria Guarnaschelli, senior editor at William Morrow and Company, for her persistent good sense, tough advice, and creative suggestions, all of which helped shape the book for your easier reading and use.

Bruce Giffords, copyeditor at William Morrow, for his masterful editing of the text, which saved it time and again from the very errors it proscribes.

Gerard F. McCauley, our literary agent, for his good counsel and Job-like patience, not to mention sense of humor.

The many students at Harvard who read and used early drafts of the book, for their sharp criticisms and helpful suggestions, not to mention *their* senses of humor.

Finally, Kate Eyre, mutual friend, whose introduction of the co-authors three years ago led to this collaboration.

While the copyright for Carol Austin Bridgewater's essay is in the name of Condé Nast, the publisher and author have made every effort to locate her in order to secure her permission to reprint it in this book. The authors would appreciate her contacting them at her convenience.

—V. A. Howard
J. H. Barton
Harvard University

Contents

Introduction

IN BRIEF

Most books on writing assume that the sole aim of writing is communication. Communication is surely an important objective of writing but not the only one, nor the first. We take a differing view that the first goal of writing, like reading, is to understand; only then can one make that understanding available to others in writing. Thinking in writing is, in fact, a form of understanding—a way of shaping first thoughts—whereas communicating in writing is mostly a matter of *re*-shaping our thoughts on paper. In brief, from first thoughts to the last word in writing, *articulation precedes communication.*

One's conceptions of the activity of writing, of the purposes it serves, and of how to do it better are substantially altered by this difference in perspective. Especially affected is the age-old problem of "getting it all down on paper" or "writer's block" engendered by the tendencies to separate thinking from writing, on the one hand, and, on the other, to make a single desperate attempt to "get it all right." If this little book helps get you over that hump alone, its existence is justified.

This is both an old and a new approach to writing better, because of the mixture of traditional and contemporary perspectives. What is traditional is the stress given to the unity of clear thinking, correct English usage, and effective expression. That has its roots in the ancient *trivium* of logic, grammar, and rhetoric. Historically, they have come apart and are nowadays treated separately, as witness the many books on writing that deal only cursorily with reasoning and the equally many logic texts that never mention writing. Reasoning, writing, and expression belong together, and here they are reunited. The contemporary influence on this book comes from recent developments in the theory of symbols (semiotics), which stress the role of symbolic systems, including language of course, as *instruments* of thought and perception—as the mind's tools. Hence, the title *Thinking on Paper* is to be taken quite literally, for that is what you will learn from this book.

Oscar Wilde said, "To be intelligible is to be found out," a remark that captures the essence of writing both as an action you do and as a result you achieve. The idea is to learn to think in writing primarily for your own edification and then for the eyes of others. This approach will enable you to use writing to become more intelligible to yourself— to find your meaning—as well as to communicate effectively with others—to be found out.

HOW TO USE THIS BOOK

This is both a reference and a guide book to writing improvement, combining *what* with *how to.* You might think of it as a "companion" to better writing. It presupposes that you are writing on demand for study, government, or business and that you would like to write more efficiently and better than you now do. It further supposes that you want to accomplish that goal quickly and in a way that applies directly to your current work with a minimum of fuss, without a lot of exercises to do before getting down to your own pressing work.

Accordingly, we have divided the book into two main parts: Part I, "Writing for Thinking," and Part II, "Thinking for Writing." Part I mainly concerns the activity of writing itself: what it is; how to get (and keep) going; how to generate, collect, and collate ideas; how to compose an essay or research paper. Part II concerns the arts of reasoning and of correct English usage: the tools of reasoning and how to apply them; how to structure arguments; how to convince rationally and persuasively; how to use grammar and punctuation.

We suggest that you first peruse the Table of Contents and decide on either of two routes through this book, reflecting its two uses as a guide or as a reference. If you are scared stiff about your next writing task, begin at the beginning, using the book as a writing "coach." Think of it as a friendly adviser offering you suggestions and hints borne of painful experience. (The authors' controlling conceit throughout was "I wish someone had told me this twenty years ago!") If you feel moderately secure in your current writing task, begin with whatever topic catches your eye first and branch out from there following your major concerns. For instance, if you have some training in logic, you might even begin with Appendix A just to refresh your grasp of the subject.

The observations and explanations, advice and illustrations given here vary widely as regards what you can do with them. Remember that this is not an elementary text or workbook. Everything herein is something directly applicable to your current or next writing task. Some chapters, like Chapters 1 (on writing and thinking) and 4 (on making sense), recommend a way of looking at writing or reasoning intended to liberate you from certain inhibiting preconceptions. Others are more "how to" in nature, like Chapters 2 (on the writing process), 3 (on essay writing), 5 (on reasoning strategies), and 6 (on punctuation and grammar). Throughout, we will try to keep you alerted as to the nature of the material being presented—an explanation, an illustration, a bit of strategy or advice—and how best to use it.

PART I

WRITING
FOR THINKING

CHAPTER 1

Writing Is Thinking

WRITER'S ANGST

Who among us when confronted with a difficult writing task has not said, "I have all the ideas but simply cannot find the right words to express them"? Or "I know my stuff, but I cannot organize my ideas clearly and convincingly"? Or "I have trouble communicating my thoughts on paper"? Many people shy away from writing for such reasons. If you are one of them, take heart. Practical writing is less a matter of mystery than of mastery of skills, many of which you already possess.

Why, then, do so many people find writing difficult? For one thing, it *is* difficult, but so are many tasks we readily learn to do well. For another, the handbooks of grammar, composition, and style mostly tell us what to do but not how to do it. However, an even greater obstacle to writing improvement is our tendency to dwell on either the final results or the mental origins of writing to the exclusion of the activity of writing, as if an empty gap separated writing from thinking.

We are understandably concerned with results, with writing that communicates well. But when that preoccupation combines with the popular notion that writing ability is a "gift" or inborn talent, the effect is to cloak the activity of writing in false mystery. Add to the pot the mistaken belief that good writers find "just the right words right away," and the mystery is complete. Little wonder that writing takes on the proportions of a quixotic quest. On the other hand, eliminate the mystery and the way is open to writing mastery for virtually any practical purpose. This means ridding yourself of misconceptions about writing that seriously inhibit the effort to do it.

The first step is to get clear in your mind what writing is, and what it isn't. The second step is to get you going in a way that frees your intelligence and imagination from the oppressive weight of searching for "just the right words." Those are the objectives of the remainder of this and the next chapter respectively.

THINKING IN WRITING: THREE PROPOSITIONS

Understanding the nature of the task is crucial to getting started in writing as in anything. Three propositions help to explain the complex relations among writing, thinking, and communicating. They are:

1. Writing is a symbolic activity of meaning-making;
2. Writing for others is a staged performance; and
3. Writing is a tool of understanding as well as of communication.

Together these add up to the claim that writing is "thinking on paper" in which both writer and reader are witnesses to meaning-in-the-making, a meaning that the writer creates and the reader attempts to re-create. Each of these propositions clarifies different aspects of how we think in writing.

Proposition 1: Writing is a symbolic activity of meaning-making.

Symbols are essential to any process of meaning-making, including writing. The fact bears mention, for many people are unaccustomed to think of letters, words, or language as such as consisting of symbols, perhaps because speech itself appears to be "second nature." To others, the word *symbol* connotes the idea of obscure meaning, meaning that is esoteric or hidden, requiring special training or sensitivity to understand. Examples of the latter would include poetic images, religious icons, the hidden meanings of dreams, or the "body language" of gestures.

Symbols can be either special, like the aforementioned, or quite commonplace. In fact, the word *symbol* applies to anything that carries meaning, usually by standing for something else: like the word *cat* in English or *gato* in Spanish. So the realm of symbolism in the prosaic sense of the term encompasses words, languages generally, and a host of other kinds of symbols: maps, road signs, gestures, diagrams, pictures, and the like (cf. Goodman, 1972; Howard, 1982).

Symbols mediate not only communication but thought itself, and language is our most common symbolic tool to think with: silently, aloud, or in writing to ourselves or to others. Certainly we do not create the world with our symbols, but whatever the world comes to *mean* to us is literally a symbolic achievement. And the meanings we attach to things and events outside ourselves shape us in turn, including how we think, feel, act, and react. We grasp what our grasp of symbols enables us to grasp.

Practically, this means that communication in writing is never perfect and seldom complete. Perfect communication in the sense of direct transmission of meaning from one mind to another (telepathy) never occurs in writing. Writing is always *mediated thought,* thought that is embodied in an intervening structure of language. Communication is seldom complete except in very simple statements like "Go left!" or "It's raining," and even those can misfire if the context is unclear. "Go left!" at the next interesection or politically? "It's raining," outdoors or in my heart?

You as a writer create a tapestry of linguistic symbols on paper that enable your reader to unravel your meaning as best he or she can. You cannot communicate your meaning except as you articulate it *and* your reader re-creates it via the medium of language. Of course, there are no guarantees that you will fully articulate your meaning or that your reader will fully grasp it. Success or failure can occur on either side.

Attending to these simple facts helps lay to rest two inhibiting preconceptions about writing; namely, that it aims solely at communication (ignoring articulation), and that such communication should be perfect and complete. Both engender the self-defeating quest to get it right the first time, perhaps the single greatest "block" to getting started.

Proposition 2: Writing for others is a staged performance.

Writing becomes a staged performance the moment you as writer become aware of a possible audience (including your later self). You should not think of writing as performing, however, until you are ready to. Up to that point, writing is a private activity of thinking on paper, a relatively unselfconscious effort to shape your thoughts without any intention to share them as such. No sooner do you ask how the words look or sound, or step back to criticize their gist, than you are performing. Therein lies the difference between free-flowing articulation and critical *revision* directed at communicating your ideas. The complete discipline of writing requires both uninhibited articulation and critical revision of one's first thoughts. Or, to put it another way, second thoughts on paper are *edited* thoughts for others' eyes.

Psychologically, we shift back and forth from one state of

mind to the other, from the struggle to articulate to the struggle to communicate. Often, the two are combined in fluent speech and writing, but the difference between writing for yourself and writing for others is crucial to taking control of the writing process. That is because discovering, articulating, and formulating ideas is not the same as criticizing, testing, and reshaping them. Flexing these skills separately eliminates the conflicts among them while enhancing their coordination in the final result (cf. Elbow, 1981, pp. 6ff).

Nearly always, a moment comes in the writer's odyssey when discovery and criticism recombine in a single effort. That is when you use your awareness of a potential audience to shake up your generative, critical, and expressive capacities all at once. In that way, like a well-rehearsed stage presentation, writing becomes performing. But it is crucial for efficiency in the early stages of writing to be able to *turn off* your audience awareness, to separate writing for discovery from writing critically for presentation. This is because discovery and criticism are often mutually disruptive, originating in different mental attitudes and having different objectives.

Discovery connotes exploration, speculation, intuition, imagination, risk taking, a suspension of doubt, a headlong plunge down new corridors of thought and experience. Criticism, on the other hand, connotes cool detachment, doubt, skepticism, testing, rigorous assessments of logic and evidence. Above all, criticism differs from discovery in its ruthless penchant for rejection. Together, they represent the True Believer and the Doubting Thomas within us—two mighty antagonists not easily appeased at the same time.

Proposition 3: Writing is a tool of understanding as well as of communication.

As mentioned at the outset, communication is surely an important objective of writing but not the only one, nor the first. The first goal of writing, like reading, is to understand; only then can one make that understanding available to readers. In other words, writing as much as silent language is an instrument to think *with*—a symbolic tool for articulating ideas, indeed, the father to thought itself.

The fact that our private scribblings may be unintelligible to others as they stand, or even to ourselves later on, should not obscure their invaluable use as *thoughtful* scribblings. This is not to underrate the importance of writing that communicates well, but, rather, to underscore the fact that writing—the act of writing itself—can span the painful gap so many people feel between first thoughts and their final expression on paper. Second thoughts about first thoughts are much easier to formulate when both exist on paper. Think of it this way: Editing presupposes a text to edit.

Putting articulation before communication also reminds us that whether thinking silently, aloud, or in writing, we do not so much send our thoughts in pursuit of words as *use words to pursue our thoughts*. Later, by revising the words that first snared our thoughts, we may succeed in capturing the understanding of others.

THE COMMUNICATION FETISH

Earlier, we quoted Oscar Wilde: "To be intelligible is to be found out," a remark that neatly snares the essence of what writing is. Writing both articulates and communicates if it is intelligible, but it is precisely the *dual* nature of writing that is obscured by subsuming so much of it under the label of "communication." This is a little piece of theory worth getting straight; for, as said, what you think writing is (or isn't) can profoundly affect how you do it.

The main trouble with the writing-as-communication idea

is that it is a half-truth parading as a whole truth. It over-looks writing's first meaning-making or articulation phase, which is so crucial to getting started. The effect is like standing helpless, tools in hand, beside a flat tire with no idea of how the jack works.

Writing as communication also carries two further inhibiting suggestions: first, that thinking always precedes writing in two stages—of thinking now and finding the "right" words later; and second, that "genuine" or "real" writing is the public, final expression rather than the personal instrument of thought (cf. Trimble, 1975, p. 15). No better recipe for so-called writer's block could be devised, for it aggravates the worst of perfectionist tendencies to try to get everything right the first time. Half-truths die hard, however, and do a lot of damage before they do; so let us briefly examine how premature stress on communication frustrates the very effort to write.

DON'T WAIT FOR THE MUSE

We have already noted how writing as communication tends to drive a false wedge between thinking and writing. An especially paralyzing corollary of that separation is the notion that the Muse resides somewhere in the "unconscious," and that you must wait for *it* to act rather than yourself prodding, probing, and producing. The Muse is supposed to work behind the scenes, secretly manipulating conscious awareness and suddenly dispensing gifts of gab.

In this widely accepted view, writing is usually seen to be the outcome of "incubation"—passive unconscious thinking—or "inspiration" in the form of sudden flashes of insight. No doubt, such things happen, but it is debilitating to rely upon them. Writing is an activity, something you do, not something that "happens" to you. Waiting for the Muse to act *for* you easily becomes an excuse for not writing and the natural ally of procrastination—your blood enemy as a writer.

From a practical point of view, both incubation and inspiration are better seen as the rewards for making an effort, not the secret puppeteers of hand and mind. Anyway, incubation occurs, if at all, when you are *not* working, in periods of rest or reverie (Perkins, 1981, pp. 38–40). By and large, we invoke ideas like inspiration and incubation when we don't know what pushed us this way or that, or, having done well, we wish to cloak our achievements in mysterious origins. It's not that we are deliberately deceitful; rather, these are the throwaway explanations that most readily come to hand.

This is not to say that concepts of the unconscious, of inspiration, of incubation, or of imagination are vacuous. Rather, they are so full of different meanings as to be useless and misleading when casually invoked to explain "creative" or merely thoughtful activities: useless because they explain nothing, and misleading because they nudge us towards false conceptions of what we are doing.

Nor is this to belabor a point, for the communication fetish and its distortions afflict not only popular thinking about writing but the instructional literature as well. It can make nonsense of otherwise good advice. For example, in his otherwise excellent book *Writing with Style* (1975), J. R. Trimble speaks of "unconscious writing"—the kind that amounts to "simply putting thoughts on paper." Trimble contrasts that sort of writing with "genuine writing," where the writer is attempting to communicate with an audience. When writing unconsciously, the writer, he says, is "not writing at all; he's merely communing privately with himself."

First off, such writing is not at all "unconscious." Rather, it is deliberately *writing one's mind* as the thoughts occur. Or, to reverse the point, such writing is no more unconsciously driven than any other thinking to oneself. Neither is it any less "genuine" than writing for others. But being of the opinion that "all writing is communication" (p. 16), Trimble is led to explain writing for oneself as somehow less genuine, less real, less conscious, than writing for others. Better no explanation than one that describes those crucially important first thoughts on paper as "not writing at all." Trimble is not alone in his opinions. The majority of writing manuals offer similarly one-sided accounts of writing that fail to square with the advice on how to do it.

To conclude these preliminary remarks on the nature of writing: The practical importance of them to you as a writer is, first, to provide you with a coherent working conception of what it is to write; second, to outline the broad strategy of thinking in writing for yourself as well as for others; and third, to eliminate the most common misconceptions standing between you and the task itself. With this orientation in mind, you are ready to begin.

CHAPTER 2

From First to Last Draft: Generating, Composing, and Expressing Ideas

Initially, thinking in writing is the practice of writing things down as you go, as you think things through. That includes note taking, marginalia, shopping lists, personal reflections (as in a diary or journal), calculations and diagrams, queries and ideas jotted down in haste on scraps or envelopes, and so forth. Feelings and attitudes, values and wishes, all figure prominently in such scribblings. Indeed, thinking in writing is anything set down to help you to remember, organize, relate, deduce, explain, question, or express—any thinking on paper that aids your understanding of the topic at hand.

No doubt you have plenty of practice at this, but you may not have seen it as a vital first step in a continuous process of generation, composition, and expression. Many people find writing difficult because they try to do all three at once in a desperate attempt to get their ideas out and down, logically organized, and nicely presented in a single effort. Beginning now, think of writing as falling into roughly three *successive* phases of generating, composing, and expressing ideas.

GENERATING IDEAS

For purposes of guiding you along, we assume that you already have at least a vague notion of a topic or subject area: taxation, foreign policy, your aunt Maude or uncle Metternich. In your very next writing task, large or small, begin by thinking in writing in whatever way suits you: notes, lists of crucial terms, questions, reminders, etc. Try to write in whole sentences, or at least in whole phrases, along with the diagrams, arrows, formulas, and other devices used to get your thoughts down. As observed already, this is one of the best ways not only to preserve but to *discover* and to *identify* your thoughts. You hardly know what they are until you see them.

Thinking in writing is less a matter of finding just the right words than of using the ones at hand and letting the rest find you. For instance, the jottings below were the raw material for the paragraph immediately following:

What do we mean that writing is finding ideas? Something like capturing them as they fly through your mind. Not falling prey to the temptation to get everything right from the start. Not assuming that ideas have to be worked out complete in the head first—before anything can be put down on paper. Also, too much goes on in the head to remember it all. Result: mental paralysis.

To say that writing is finding ideas simply means putting words on paper rather than leaving them in the head. It means *not* trying to correctly formulate everything in advance. Ordinarily, when we think a problem through, we are assailed by many confusing, half-formed ideas, feelings, doubts, associations, and objections. The sheer speed and number of them becomes a burden on the memory. If they are not quickly set down, much that is valuable will be lost, and just as much that is nonsense will go undetected. The inevitable result is confusion and paralysis.

So, write on and on until you feel a flow of ideas onto the page. Consume space. Think of it that way. You should write until you feel that *too much* material has been accumulated ever to be used. Never avoid a conflict: Record both sides in "pro and con" fashion: "Sometimes I see it this way, sometimes that way." Use stock beginnings to keep your pen moving, e.g., "My thinking on this topic is . . ." or "My feelings about this are . . ." *Then write the next thought that comes into your head no matter how silly.* Ideas have a way of adding up to something only dimly perceived at the moment of their articulation.

Enjoy the headlong rush of ideas; and when those moments of lucidity come, "perform" before your imagined audience for all you are worth, *but don't stop when they pass.* Just drop back to thinking solely for yourself to the exclusion of any audience. Set aside any worries about what others might think about what you have written by reminding yourself that these private notes are for no one's eyes but your own. Let your mind roam over the topic in any direction jabbing at, alluding to, and nailing down ideas as they occur to you. Heap them up in great piles of paper and prose to the point where so much stuff is "there" that *something* can be made of it all.

Besides stock beginnings to keep your pen moving, it may help to focus your thinking to keep the following "leading questions" in mind:

A. What do I want my readers to know?
B. What do I want my readers to feel?
C. What do I want my readers to do?

Focusing on the domains of knowledge, feeling, and action, these questions also form a bridge between the content of your thinking and a potential audience. Where the topic and target audience are relatively clear to begin with, as in an assigned essay or office memo, these questions are as useful for generating ideas as for composing and criticizing them later on. They help to keep you and your audience in touch.

As for those situations where you hardly know where to start, the aim is to use writing to learn more about the subject and how to approach it. A sample of the sorts of question you might pursue to orient yourself includes the following: How do I feel about this assignment? How difficult is it? What should I read? Whom should I consult? Who is my audience? (Then plug in the questions about audience above.) What are my strengths and weaknesses? How can I best present the issue? As a balanced argument? As a plea? A pitch? In a formal or informal manner? In a who-what-how-when-where journalistic format? As a crisp bulletin or announcement? In a come-let-us-reason-together approach? All this you can profitably think about in writing as a way of avoiding blocks and of learning about your topic before writing about it directly.

Whatever you do to cut into your material during this initial phase, think "quantity" and let quality take care of itself (cf. Elbow, 1981, p. 254). "Quality" at this stage refers to whatever is adequate to capture and record your thoughts, not to their presentational quality. After all, the more you write now, the more there is to edit later on. The more false leads, poor ideas and expressions you discard, the more questions and objections you can anticipate. As well, through sheer scribbling you will begin to discover new relations, perspectives, and formulations, and not a few gems that will survive unscathed to the final draft.

Continue scribbling until you feel that repetition has set in to the point of no further returns on the investment of time and energy. Mind you, repetition is an excellent way of turning over an issue, of getting perspective through refinement, so be sure that nothing new is coming down the mental sluices before breaking off.

Take a break—a fairly long one if you can afford it. If time presses, divide the time available into thirds: a third for generation, a third for composition, and a third for final editing and style. If you are writing to a deadline, or under pressure, that simple division of effort will save you much grief.

COMPOSING IDEAS

Composing ideas falls into two parts: the *topical* draft, focusing on subject matter, and the *sequential* draft, focusing on the connections between topics.

The Topical Draft

After a rest (if you can afford it), collect all your pages and number them consecutively. Now begins the composition phase—a first phase of criticism that stresses order, structure, organization. *Read over your notes, sorting them according to topic.* Treat this as an exercise in the *labeling of paragraphs or pages,* a matter of putting titles to large and small chunks of prose that seem to dwell on a single topic. The label might be a single word, a longer title, a question addressed. For example, looking back over the preceding four significant paragraphs, one might label them respectively: "Quantity versus quality," "Repetition," "When to quit: time division," and "Topic labeling." Here you have the basis of a primitive (but useful!) information retrieval system.

Using a differently colored ink or pencil is a good way of keeping track of the difference between your raw prose and the new labels, marginalia, and remarks. Simply underlining the topic labels is another highlighting device. Don't worry about the sequence of topics just yet, unless it comes easily or appears obvious. Merely say in a word or two what each chunk of prose is about. *Use the same headings when you come back to a topic,* or alter them slightly to indicate a new wrinkle, e.g., "When to quit: taking breaks." What emerges from this are the *elements of an outline* that gradually puts itself together with far less pain and frustration than trying to do it in advance of writing anything would.

You may find yourself adding, amending, elaborating on the raw prose as you would in taking notes on your readings. Do this *quickly,* however, keeping these secondary notes simple and separate, as marginalia to the original text. Occasionally, when you feel like it, write addenda to the original text on the backs of the same sheets. Or, if you prefer, insert additional sheets and number them with *a*'s and *b*'s— 2a, 2b, and so forth—to indicate where they should go. Ignore the messiness; anything that enables you to keep track is fine.

Labeling your ideas will take some time, and many new ideas will occur to you as you do it, precisely because you now have a text before you to reflect upon, to react to, and to amend. Be tough-minded and as specific as you can both in your labeling and in your marginalia. *Root the following questions in your mind: What am I saying here? What is my point? What is my problem? What is my solution? What shall I call this chunk of words?*

Note that these questions keep you focused on whatever is on the page while stimulating you to further reflection. Rehearse them over and over, especially when you feel confused, disoriented, or distracted. After all, your reader will ask the very same questions of your final text. By asking them of yourself and your own rough text, you are taking the first step toward getting in touch with your eventual reader. (What do I want the reader to know?) Psychologically, however, you are still aiming to satisfy yourself first.

Take another break. Remind yourself of your accomplishments: a mountain of raw prose, some additions and modifications, topic headings amounting to the elements of an outline. Do something else now like ironing or walking the dog, something that allows you to muse on your ideas without pressure. The aim is to distract yourself but not completely, to live with your ideas without the pressure of full concentration (which is quite different from sleeping on them, as we shall see in a moment).

Reading back over your raw prose again, you will observe that large chunks belong together under a single heading and perhaps a few subheadings. As well, your marginal remarks and queries will have added considerably to the content and to a growing sense of organization (including what to get rid of). Your categories, represented by the labeled headings, will develop relations among themselves, some of which will seem quite obvious or to form a natural sequence. Some pieces will seem out in left field, but just set them aside and concentrate on the elements that fall naturally into place.

The next step is to rewrite the original with minimal corrections except for including your annotations and collecting the separate pieces of raw prose under your headings. That is, whereas you might have several sections labeled, say, "History of the problem," put them all together in any order whatever under that heading.

A note on technology here: If you have been writing by hand on lined sheets (better than unlined ones for reducing messiness), you may want to shift over to the typewriter or word processor at this point. Both will give you a neater text to work with. Besides neatness, there is the reward of seeing your new, growing text emerge from the chaos of scattered notes. If you have been using a typewriter or word processor from the start, simply retype the original or print out the original before retyping it on the word processor. It is easier, incidentally, to do your annotating and labeling on a print-out, where you can put arrows, numbers, and tiny remarks in the margins, than it is to keep scrolling back and forth on the screen. Besides, you will need to see your pages spread out before you for ease of scanning.

As you retype, cross out the raw prose sections, paragraph by paragraph. This will help you to keep track of things, since you will be hopping from page to page to collect widely scattered items under their appropriate headings. Also, the combination of crossing out the original raw prose and the more organized, quick growth of the rewrite are incentives to your work. You can *see* your progress as old paragraphs are discarded and new ones emerge.

Continue rewriting until all but the most obviously useless or fragmentary material has been topically arranged. *Think of rewriting at this stage as mainly retyping even though more than that is happening.* It is important that you retype your material, even if you're mostly copying out the original, for small but cumulative changes, corrections, and linking phrases will occur to you as you go along. That way, you reengage your material, *converting the static record of your previous thought into active thinking.* By retyping you will be doing more than merely shifting prose blocks about scissors-and-paste style.

Let the aforementioned subtle changes occur, but don't press for them. If anxiety to organize mounts, remind yourself that this is a mostly "mechanical," second-stage cleanup operation—a matter of putting things in their proper places for convenient access. Inevitably, the results will be more than that, but, *to keep the pressure off and the production rate up, think of this as a "shuffling procedure," like sorting cards according to suit.*

Take another break if time permits. After all, you have been *working.* Enjoy the feeling of productivity, of knowing that you can build a mountain of useful prose. And remember that the utility of much of it lies in your ruthless capacity to get rid of a lot of it. Rejecting the "junk" will sharpen your wits about what works and what doesn't. By now you will have accumulated enough material to do that with confidence, free from the twin specters of running out of things to say or being locked into a single viewpoint or meager set of ideas. Any number of alternatives lie right there on the pages before you awaiting your scrutiny and choice. You are far from finished, *but you have broken the back of your writing task: You have a first draft!*

The Sequential Draft

Now go back over this topically organized first draft making further marginal notes but this time *trying to discover a natural, commonsense sequence, or set of sequences, among the topics.* Many of the main points will leap out at you as you peruse the pages. Mark them as such: "leading idea," "supporting evidence," "conclusion," and the like. A definitive statement may suggest itself as capturing the essence of this or that section. Write it into the text. Using numerals, arrows, or any other convenient marks, group what appear to you to be subordinate passages under the main ones; again, with the idea in mind that they should eventually form a series of points as in giving directions, presenting information or evidence, or making a court case.

For instance, your first draft might contain a list of headings like the following:

Practical implications of the problem
Current reactions to the problem
History of the problem
Exact nature of the problem
Recommendations
Solutions to the problem

These headings and their order reflect the order of your original thinking, your private train of thought. Because of your background, training, interests, knowledge, and experience, your mind traveled certain idiosyncratic paths productive of your ideas. Everyone has his or her own way of mulling over an issue, even if certain conventions of reasoning and expression tend to govern the process. (See Chapter 4, "Making Sense.") Now, however, you have to think about what arrangement of your ideas will best communicate them to a target audience. The order of your thinking and the order of its most effective presentation are not necessarily the same.

The first things to ask yourself here are, Who are my readers? What do they expect? What do I want them to know, to feel, to do? Let's assume that the aforementioned problem concerns industrial pollution of inland waterways in the Great Lakes area. You have been assigned the task of writing a report for an investigating agency of the federal government. Assuming knowledge to be the agency's prime interest, a natural topic sequence might be this one:

The nature and extent of industrial pollution in the designated area
The history of the problem
Current reactions to industrial pollution
Practical implications of the problem
Solutions to the problem
Specific recommendations

The headings might be shifted about depending upon whether the main interests of your audience are "political," "scientific," or "mercantile." The sequence above is appropriate for an investigating agency primarily interested in the problem, its origins, and attitudes toward it. In some kinds of business writing, however, recommendations tend to be put closer to the front of a document along with their "benefits, costs, and risks." Whatever sequence you choose, simply number the headings in a rough series being careful to note in the margins the *connections* among the several items. Certain connecting phrases like "This suggests . . . ," "Moreover . . . ," "But consider the opposite case . . . ," "On the other hand . . . ," will help seal these relations for yourself as well as for the reader.

You are now well along in the compositional phase of writing, your critical faculties transforming the landscape of your document to make it easier to traverse. *This sequential revision is your second draft, even before retyping, where writer-centered concerns give way to reader-centered concerns.*

After this first try at reordering the labeled items, it is advisable to set the document aside for a while in order to gain some distant perspective on it. Now is the time to sleep on the text if at all possible. That simply means distancing yourself from it sufficiently to see your work as a reader might and to give yourself leeway for new points and information to occur to you.

EXPRESSING IDEAS

When again you take up the manuscript, your main concern is expression and communication (note how many steps come before this phase!): matters of format, style, grammar, tone, accessibility, and the like. *For now, think of this as performance time, a time to put yourself "onstage," as earlier described.* Imagine you are ready to make a formal presentation to your target audience; adopt a persona if you like—play the role; above all, try to take the situation in which you and your document must perform *into your own mind.* That means taking account also of the possible opposition to your views.

Incorporating the new order and stray marginalia, review the manuscript again but with primary attention to making your ideas accessible, understandable, sharp, persuasive. You may find that whole passages are fine as they are, so a bit of "scissors and paste" will save you extra effort at this stage (particularly if you are using a word processor). *But remember that rewriting, however mechanical it feels, is rethinking, and this is a crucial stage of rethinking for external consumption.*

Imagine your reader asking for clarifications, objecting reasonably, objecting *wrongly,* wanting to know the point of it all, where it is all leading. *Live this experience on the page as you rewrite,* answering the audience's requests for direction and clarification as you go: How does this connect to that? What do you mean by this? As before, *write your mind, but now to that person or audience.*

If you are still uneasy about getting through to your audience, you might try delivering a mock lecture. Use a tape recorder if it doesn't inhibit you, or rehearse the whole thing before a mirror. Anything that gets you "in touch," creates a sense of rapport, is legitimate now: any device, conceit, fantasy, or fear. Even fear can be useful, especially that variety called butterflies, the kind that accompanies confidence and the willingness to take a plunge.

You may want to pause occasionally this time through to make sure that you are meeting your audience's demands or to capture that wonderful metaphor or bon mot. But again, don't wait too long (too long is whenever you feel stuck). Immediately when you feel stalled, get up, walk around ("offstage"), have another cup of coffee; then make another "entrance" onto your mental stage. *It is important throughout the writing process that the changes you feel obliged to make are small ones to avoid being stalled for long—unless of course big ones are coming easily, in which case, make them.*

By now you are thinking in writing for others and entering an advanced stage of revision. It is advisable to sleep on this third draft too, preferably for a few days if the document is especially important or difficult. *Then read over the manuscript aloud listening to how it sounds.* Play the reader, and make further deletions, additions, and corrections as they occur to you just then. You will be amazed at how many small but important changes will pop out at you.

You have some further options at this stage to improve your text. You may have it critiqued by someone whose knowledge of grammar and style is equal to or better than your own. You may request a "sympathetic critic" to suggest ways of strengthening the arguments and content. Or, you can go all out and submit your text to a known hostile critic so as to anticipate the most vehement objections. Interestingly, sympathetic critics often come up with the most substantial and penetrating criticisms, since they too want the document to work, are sensitive to why it may not, but are less inclined to take cheap shots. Having done as much as you can, now is the time to let your document go, to live its own life (as it will anyway).

We have taken you on a three-draft tour of writing strategy designed especially for those who must write on demand. Nobody has a monopoly on *the* writing process, and everybody goes about it in different ways at different times for different purposes. Still, the procedure outlined above is a proven effective way, particularly for those having difficulty getting started and organizing a lot of material.

Some pieces of writing will come easier, telescoping some of the steps recommended. Longer writing chores, like books, large reports, and theses, will pass through several more drafts in part or whole. Three is average for most medium-length documents—letters, memorandums, essays, journal articles, and the like. Basically, however, the procedures and the experience of writing are fairly much the same whether you achieve the desired results in one draft, three drafts, or ten. Writing is like prospecting. Sometimes we make a lucky find of a nugget lying on the surface, but most of the time it takes a lot of sifting to find the precious metal in the sand.

A final note on monitoring your progress. Writing is in fact a continuous process of generation, composition, and expression in which all of its phases are repeated over and over and sometimes combined (as in the last stages of revision). As well, you will find yourself slipping or skipping from one phase to another, sometimes to good effect, sometimes not. To avoid the blocks and confusion that come from trying to do too much at once or reaching too soon for final results, *be aware of where you are in the writing process; and as much as possible treat generation, composition, and expression as sequential phases of writing*. That way you can focus your energies and attention with the least pain for the maximum results.

CHAPTER 3

The Essay: A Framework for Thinking in Writing

THE FUNCTION OF FORMATS

Remember all those themes, essays, and term papers you had to write in school or college? What possessed your teachers to send you reeling over the years from "My Summer Holidays" to "Slickensiding in Silurian Sediments"? Why is the essay format so widely used for instructional purposes? The answer lies less in the variable contents, obviously, than in the format, the logical structure of the essay itself. As an exercise in information collection, the organization of ideas, explanation, and argumentation, the essay is not only a versatile pedagogical device but a powerful tool for discovery and communication. Indeed, the essay is the simplest, most basic format for discursive writing—writing intended to inform, to explain, or to persuade.

From both writers' and readers' points of view, the essay is a framework for thinking in writing employing every strategy of reasoning, weighing of evidence, and persuasion required for virtually any subject or discipline. It is not too much to say that the essay format is *the* basic structure for making sense to others on paper. Whatever the specific format—the business report, book review, newspaper editorial, scientific or scholarly paper—the elements of the traditional essay recur again and again in different guises.

Mastery of the basic elements of the essay will quite literally liberate your thinking on a topic by making it accessible to others as well as giving formal direction to the processes of generation, composition, and expression described in the preceding chapter.

Many useful guides to essay writing exist, but none that present the essay format as a natural extension of thinking and reasoning. Most guides approach the essay as a schoolish device for structuring and communicating the results of prior thinking—a kind of literary packaging of the finished products of thought. In fact, essays *grow;* they expand, contract, and change shape with the thinking that goes into them. Until the last change of wording and the last punctuation mark, your thinking in writing is not finished. From the writer's standpoint, then, the essay is more like a flexible framework within which to think and to communicate than a rigid box into which thinking's results are compressed.

We need an example now for case study. Reproduced below is a typical sample of essay writing of the kind found in popular magazines. The paragraphs are numbered for convenient reference; the other marks will be explained later on. For the moment, read through the article as you normally would, concentrating on its content.

THE BAD NEWS ABOUT LOOKING TOO GOOD
By Carol Austin Bridgwater
Mademoiselle, May 1981

1. If you could snap your fingers and be absolutely gorgeous . . . would you? Before you decide, consider this: While there are definite advantages to being beautiful, there are also some very real drawbacks. In fact, the more average-looking among us may be just as well off in the end.

2. First, the advantages of beauty. Way back in 1966, Dr. Elaine Hatfield, a sociologist at the University of Wisconsin, and her colleague Dr. Ellen Berscheid, studied dating preferences of college freshmen who attended a dance with blind dates of varying levels of attractiveness. After the dance, the researchers found, the attractive women tended to be asked out again, and the good-looking dates of both sexes were reported to be better-liked than the average or unattractive dates. Intelligence and social skills didn't seem to count for much.

3. Other researchers have demonstrated that both men and women assume that attractive people are more sensitive, kind, warm, and sexually responsive than unattractive people. And they were thought to lead more exciting lives and have more prestigious careers. "This is a stereotype that's held by virtually everyone—men and women, young and old," says Dr. Mark Snyder, a psychologist at Stanford University's Center for Advanced Study in the Behavioral Sciences, in Palo Alto, California.

4. But before you give up all hope because you've never been mistaken for Miss America, there's a twist to Dr. Snyder's story. He did an experiment in which men talked over the phone to women they had never met. Men who were *told* that they were talking to attractive women were much more warm and outgoing in their conversations than men who thought they were talking to uglies. What's fascinating is that, in spite of the fact that all the women were equally attractive, the "beauties" responded by being more confident and animated than the "uglies." Snyder explains, "Once we categorize people as either attractive or unattractive, we unknowingly influence them to behave according to our expectations."

5. And while that doesn't sound altogether encouraging it is, in fact, good news. For while there are few stunners in the world whom no one could call less than

beautiful, most of us fall in a category which Snyder describes as being "attractive to some people, but not to others. Beauty is in the eye of the beholder, so to speak. When you interact with those who see you as attractive, our research shows they'll bring out the best in you."

6. What makes someone see another as "attractive"? Studies show that a man is more drawn to a woman who shares similar attitudes with him. In fact, some researchers have found that similarity in attitudes is even *more* important than looks in drawing people to one another. Other studies show that people will think you're more attractive if you make it clear that you like them and enjoy their company. Also, the more someone likes you, the more attractive you seem to him or her. Finally, then, as people get to know each other, like each other, and learn that they have things in common, their attractiveness increases in each other's eyes.

7. What this means is that even the most average-looking among us will get to be beautiful—at least sometimes! At the same time, we may well avoid some of the disadvantages of being stunning. And what, you may ask, could those possibly be?

8. In one experiment, attractive women were judged to have a number of positive traits. But they were also considered to be snobbish, materialistic and vain. Attractive women were also considered less approachable: In one experiment, men admitted that the more attractive a woman is the more they feared rejection.

9. Keep in mind, too, that the psychologists doing all this experimenting have focused primarily on how attractiveness affects first impressions in brief social encounters. Whatever edge the beautiful have, therefore, may be evened out over time. After all, in the end it's the total human being that counts in the best relationships in our lives.

THE BASIC STRUCTURE OF THE ESSAY

The essay, whatever its content, is like a skeleton consisting of three main parts: the introduction, the body, and the conclusion. However cleverly done, virtually every piece of discursive writing is constructed around that tripartite structure, rather like a song: verse, refrain, coda. For example, the standard business letter begins, "Dear Sir: I am writing to . . ." and continues, "Certainly we may . . . However, if . . . Moreover . . ." and concludes, "Therefore, might we suggest . . ." Even the humble office memo introduces its author, audience, and topic by the simple device of stereotypical headings. Like this:

> MEMORANDUM
> From: Arthur Jones
> To: All Assembly personnel
> Re: Installation of robot welders

However you do it, the topic has to be introduced, the issues and arguments presented, and the conclusions drawn or recommendations made. The most common mistake of fledgling writers is to ignore the *structural constants* of the essay (or any other format, for that matter) while plunging directly into the body *content.* That leaves the topic unintroduced, unsummarized, unconcluded, and the document itself often unread—or read unsympathetically. If that is your tendency, remember the writer's oldest saw of all: Say what you are going to do, do it, then say what you've done.

Now look back over Bridgwater's essay with these remarks in mind. Where does she say what she's going to do? Where does she do it? Where does she draw her main conclusion? The answers are perhaps obvious: paragraph 1, paragraphs 2 to 8, and paragraph 9 respectively. Being aware of the *questions* is crucial for guiding your own writing. Beyond that, the details of structure are not so obvious; and here's where we get down to the business of learning how to use the essay format.

Lucile Vaughan Payne in *The Lively Art of Writing* (1965) conveniently diagrams the essay's "bare bones of structure" as follows:

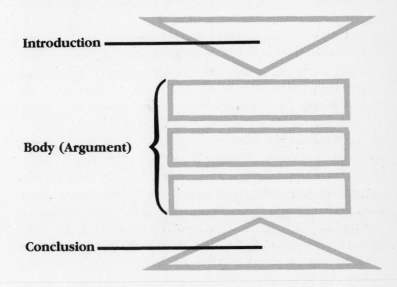

Introduction

Body (Argument)

Conclusion

Figure 1—Structure of the Essay
(reprinted with permission)

Payne explains the above diagram as follows: "Think of each of the units in Figure 1 as one paragraph. Certain obvious characteristics show up at once: (1) the first, or introductory paragraph begins broadly and narrows to a point; (2) the middle section, or 'argument,' is in block form and takes up most of the space in the essay; and (3) the last, or concluding, paragraph begins at a narrow point and ends broadly" (p. 42). We shall call this the classic model of the essay and describe how its parts are constructed and put together.

FORMULATING THE THESIS

At the logical core of the essay (and at the diagrammatic point of the introduction) is the thesis. No opinion, no thesis, no essay. It's that simple, however many facts, details, or explanations you have. The essay does not merely inform; it takes a stand. In most instances, this does not mean assuming a warlike stance or tone of shrill advocacy. Rather it means offering a rational defense and development of an opinion as precisely formulated as you can make it. Alternatively, it means raising a precise question—usually about something controversial—and attempting to answer it.

The thesis is your answer to the questions, What do I want my readers to know? To feel? To do? Or, more simply, What do I want to *say*? If you can answer that question with any degree of clarity, then you have a *working thesis*—at least enough to get going. Construing the question of what you want to say in terms of your readers' knowledge, feelings, and actions helps to focus in on your major point as well as away from what you do not want to say.

In paragraph 1, for instance,. Bridgwater's thesis comes at the end with the statement "In fact, the more average-looking among us may be just as well off in the end." That's her opinion and the view she explores and defends in the body of the essay. *The question for any writer is how to get from an initial, perhaps vague or overstated, working thesis to one that is clear and defensible.*

To show you how, imagine that you yourself wrote Bridgwater's essay and that you share her viewpoint (whether or not you do). Imagine further that you have read and consulted the same researchers on the topic and that you are struggling to formulate your central theme. How might a first stab at it look? Perhaps something like this:

A. Pretty people get too much too easily in this world. It's about time that the average-looking got a break. After all, looks aren't everything, and they sure as hell don't guarantee good character, reliability, or competence.

Fine as a gut response and a good use of strong feelings to evoke an opinion. But how does this statement stack up as a defensible thesis? Imagine the response of a deadly cool Defender of the Opposition. The statement is too accusative ("too much too easily," "It's about time"), shrill ("sure as hell"), and general ("got a break"). Presumably, your intention goes beyond preaching to the converted, to convincing the skeptical and undecided. As a rule of thumb, it is well to remember that an overly emotional statement of an opinion tends to render it less rationally defensible.

Still, you have a working thesis, something to edit and refine. Go back over the emotional words and phrases looking behind them for the grain of truth they contain. "Too much too easily": What does the research suggest are the actual advantages of being attractive? "It's about time . . . got a break": Maybe there are advantages to being average-looking too. "Sure as hell don't guarantee . . .": The research suggests that most people realize that and more, that some prejudices work against unusually attractive people. It's a relatively short step from these critical reflections to Bridgwater's own formulation:

B. While there are definite advantages to being beautiful, there are also some very real drawbacks. In fact, the more average-looking among us may be just as well off in the end.

An intermediate, longer revision of statement A incorporating the recast emotional terms might look like this:

C. Common experience and research suggests that beautiful people have definite initial advantages in life.

However, those advantages are not unmixed blessings. Being average-looking has its advantages too. Also, whether one is perceived as being attractive depends a lot on characteristics and behavior that have little to do with looks.

The longer statement C may never appear in your essay in so many words (and in fact does not appear in Bridgwater's), but it is your complete thesis—a full if somewhat laborious statement of it, taking account of the major factors involved and staking out the main lines of defense. The purpose of writing it out in full is to give yourself the strongest possible sense of direction.

Aside from strengthening your sense of direction, writing out the thesis in full protects you from having too much or too little to say. When ideas come quickly from many different angles, the tendency is to dump them all into the pot willy-nilly. On the other hand, when they come slowly, the tendency is to grasp at anything available. As Payne observes, "The full thesis . . . disciplines the writer who has too many ideas, forcing him to organize his scattered thoughts and to check each one for relevance. It stimulates the writer who has too few ideas, reminding him of the exact points that he must bring out" (p. 38).

Typically, the full thesis emerges toward the end of the generative phases of writing as you move into the compositional phase. Look for it in the piles of prose accumulated during the generative stages as you begin labeling your paragraphs. Pursue it with the question, What am I trying to say; what is my overall point, question, objective? The exact statement you will use in the essay may come much later, even during final revisions. The important thing to know in composition is *what* stand you intend to take and *where* to state it first.

WRITING THE INTRODUCTION

Perhaps the single most inhibiting demand ever made upon inexperienced writers is the demand for a detailed advance outline of the whole essay. It's like being asked to announce one's discoveries before making them. Over and again, we have stressed the notion of writing as an open-ended process of inquiry and discovery. Thinking in writing is a disciplined activity that takes on increasingly definite shape as you go along. To quote British novelist Graham Greene, "When School was safely behind me I began to write 'essays' again. I learned to trust the divagations of the mind. If you let the reins loose the horse will find its way home. The shape was something which grew *inside* the essay, during the revision—you didn't have to think it out beforehand" (1980, p. 208). Armed with a reasonably explicit thesis statement and trusting the "divagations of the mind," you are ready to write the introduction to your (i.e., Bridgwater's) essay.

While the specific details of any essay tend to follow the divagations of the mind, the overall structure is ironclad—introduction, body, and conclusion—with many of the same devices being employed over and over. For example Bridgwater's paragraph 1 begins with a general question of arresting implications ("If you could snap your fingers and be absolutely gorgeous . . . would you?"). The effect is to draw the reader onto her ground with maximum interest and minimum resistance. Then comes the cautionary note that leads on to the thesis statement at the end of the paragraph ("Before you decide . . ."). Bridgwater here follows the classic model, which is to begin broadly and quickly focus in on the main issue, like an arrow aimed at the heart of the matter.

As a practiced writer, Bridgwater draws us in with a provocative question, then a reservation, followed by the main point. But there are other ways of accomplishing the same result even if less interestingly. The idea is to get to the point as quickly as possible. For instance, a perfectly respectable beginning might run as follows:

> Most people would prefer to be more physically attractive than they are. Pretty people seem to get their way more easily in life. But being beautiful is not an unmixed blessing. In fact, the more average-looking among us may be just as well off in the end.

The point of this illustration is to emphasize that you don't have to be cute or clever to succeed. You need only be clear and succinct. In that respect, three extremes are *always* to be avoided: (a) backing into the topic; (b) barging into the topic; and (c) bungling into the topic.

Backing into the Topic

Backing into the topic results from trying to provide too much background. For example:

> Physical beauty is a great advantage in life. From the time of Helen of Troy (the face that launched a thousand ships), people have deferred to the power of physical charm. Nowadays television glorifies the "beautiful people" as idols and ideals to strive for. But as the example of Marilyn Monroe well shows, stunning beauty is not all that it's cracked up to be.

What is the point of all this background? Where is it leading? Why all the name-dropping? Why the distracting reference to television and "beautiful people"? Instead of focusing the reader on an arguable point, this rambling introduction causes the mind to wander.

Fledgling writers often approach a writing assignment this

way hoping to display their knowledge and erudition. More often, the effect is to disguise their best thinking while creating a feeling of unease in the reader who senses the lack of focus.

Barging into the topic

Thesis statement A above (p. 49) is a good example of barging in—for all the reasons given, it is not an easily defensible statement. Fine for private exploratory purposes, as a public statement it assaults rather than attracts the reader. It demands compliance, thus creating instant resistance. The heavy hand is not always the most persuasive, especially on paper.

Bungling into the Topic

Humor is one of the most difficult forms of writing in any genre and one of the easiest ways to fail. Better to avoid the "cute" beginning unless it comes quite naturally to you (as judged by others!). Some writers develop a genuine flair for the clever or shocking opener, but when it fails, it fails miserably. For instance:

> Beauty is only skin deep? Not if you've got the skin others like to touch! And who isn't a soft touch for a pretty face? Still, it's not all cake and ale for the pretty pusses.

Such an opener is certainly enough to make one's skin crawl. An odor of hucksterism hovers over the prose like a cheap perfume. Unless that is the effect one is deliberately trying to create, all sense of serious intent is destroyed. The best advice about trying to be clever is, don't fail to be funny.

As said, Bridgwater's introduction follows the classic pattern of opening general statement or question followed by a quick narrowing down to the main theme. Other routes to the same goal are equally effective. We will illustrate only one of the more popular ones. A common type of introduction to feature articles and how-to pieces begins with an illustrative narrative followed by a question or two that explicitly raises the main issue. For example:

> Nancy is a lawyer who's had a hard week. At twenty-eight she is a stunningly beautiful blonde who appears to have everything going for her: education, beauty, brains. But only yesterday Nancy was shunted aside by a prestigious client—for the second time in a week—in favor of another lawyer whom the client found "more approachable." "I'm good at my job, I'm pleasant and cheerful, what's wrong?" she asks. "It's as if they just want someone less attractive."
> Nancy's predicament is not unusual. . . .

Though the narrative opening differs from the explicit statement opening, the strategy remains the same: Set the stage quickly, then deliver the first important line. The narrative opening also illustrates yet another way to raise a thesis—as a question rather than as an assertion. Raising the thesis as a question has the advantage of promoting an atmosphere of inquiry as contrasted with, say, an attitude of contention. A question also anticipates the reader's point of view, thereby fostering identification with the writer. So long as you establish common ground and indicate your heading, the choice of openers is yours. That choice is made easier, however, if you keep in mind that the function of any introduction is just to introduce, no more and no less.

WRITING THE BODY

The body of the essay is where you elaborate and defend the thesis articulated in the introduction. The body presents the arguments and evidence that support your main contention while taking account of possible objections, counterarguments, and negative evidence. To prove the opposition wrong is not necessarily to prove your own case right (there may be another alternative), but the most persuasive essays are those that answer the opposition in the course of building a strong positive case. In other words, *the essay body weighs the arguments pro and con*.

So, the first step is to collect your arguments for and against the thesis. An easy way to do this is simply to list them briefly in phrases or sentences opposite each other on a page divided down the middle. Ignore the order of arguments for now; just list all the pro and all the con arguments together by quick reference to where they can be found in your raw prose text. Figure 2 shows how such a listing based on Bridgwater's essay might look.

Thesis: That the average-looking have as many advantages as beautiful people.

Pro	Con
Men *told* they were talking to beautiful woman more outgoing, warm; those categorized as beautiful responded more confidently, etc.	Beautiful more liked, more pursued, more popular.
	Beautiful assumed to be more sensitive, kind, sexy, warm.
Being thought beautiful brings out best.	
Similarity of interests, values, etc., determines categorization. More you're liked, more attractive you appear.	
All get to be "beautiful" some of the time.	
Beautiful women often considered vain, materialistic, etc. Force of counterpredjudice.	

Look back now to Figure 1 (p. 47) and compare it to Bridgwater's essay. Figure 1 has only three rectangles representing a short three-paragraph essay (minus introduction and conclusion). Bridgwater's essay contains seven body paragraphs. The number of paragraphs depends upon the number of main points pro and con to be made and the thoroughness with which you make them. You may want to go into more detail here, less there; but whatever the length of your paragraphs, the rule of thumb of paragraphing is: *one main idea per paragraph.* Usually, the "main idea" is broached in the opening sentence of each paragraph; see especially Bridgwater's paragraphs 2, 3, 6, and 7.

Now of course, a *main* idea may be complex or contain several subpoints. For instance, Bridgwater's paragraph 4 explores the behavior of people who think they are talking to someone attractive over the telephone and the reactions of the latter. That's not a simple idea, but she admirably compresses a lot of information into a short space. From the "twist" in Dr. Snyder's story to the influence on people who have been categorized as attractive, the separate points hang together tightly. As units, paragraphs are demicadences of thought, natural breaks in a sequence of ideas. How to make those breaks becomes clearer as we consider the ordering of arguments pro and con.

Payne suggests three rules for the ordering of arguments:

1. Make the necessary concessions to the opposition as soon as possible.
2. Devote at least one paragraph to every major *pro* argument in your full thesis statement.
3. Save your best argument for the last. [P. 49]

Before suggesting any modifications, let's see how these rules apply to Bridgwater's essay. First, where does she make concessions to the opposition? Paragraphs 2 and 3 rehearse the advantages of being beautiful with no qualifications. That way, *the con arguments are strongly and fairly presented.*

Letting an opposing position appear stronger than one's own for a few paragraphs is a powerful device to increase the impact of the counterclaims when they come. Bridgwater does just that in paragraphs 2 and 3. They provide the setup for paragraph 4, the turning point in the essay where she goes over to the offense.

A more important motive for doing justice to the opposition is increasing knowledge. In scholarly and scientific writing it is essential that care be taken to assess the strongest, not the weakest, formulation of the opposing view. Otherwise, you are left open to the charge of "straw man" argument against a misleadingly weak version of the opposition. This is equally true of some business and report writing, especially that which deals with measures for handling "worse cases." You never lose by showing respect for honest opposition.

From paragraph 4 to 8 Bridgwater follows rule 2 to the letter, devoting exactly one paragraph to each pro argument. In longer pieces, more space may be required to develop the several phases of one's case—whole sections (as in this book) or chapters. Note, for example, that Bridgwater's paragraph 7 elaborates the central meaning of the content of paragraph 6 even though 7 makes an independent point—that most of us get to be beautiful sometimes.

For most essays, rule 2 should read, "Devote at least one paragraph to each pro *and con* argument, if for no other reason than to show the reader that you are aware of the other side to the story." In very short pieces, however, it is sufficient merely to acknowledge the opposition briefly and to follow up each concession with a pro argument. Something like this: "While it can be argued that . . . nonetheless . . ." or "Certainly it is true that . . . but . . ." or "Admittedly . . . however . . ." The idea is to keep the focus on your own case while doing quick justice to the opposition. Such a strategy builds confidence in the reader and heads off any charge of oversight or neglect.

Payne's third recommendation, to save your strongest argument for last, is less reliable. The reason is that the argument that has the greatest impact is not necessarily the logically strongest. (See Chapter 5.) Logically, the content of Bridgwater's paragraphs 4 and 6 constitute the core of her case. But paragraph 9, coming on the heels of the preceding details, has perhaps the greater impact. In other words, "strength" is relative not only to logic and evidence but to the effect a given statement is likely to have depending on where it is placed. Imagine, for instance, paragraphs 9 and 4 reversed. The impact of the former would be considerably weakened and the logical force of the former diffused. As a clincher, however, paragraph 9 nicely summarizes the trend of argument up to that point.

If we had to describe the writing of the body of the essay in a few words, they would be *elaboration, illustration,* and *argumentation.*

Elaboration is spelling out the details, showing how things work, defining, clarifying, adding relevant information including examples. Notice that each of Bridgwater's paragraphs elaborates a central point whether pro or con. For instance, in paragraph 3 she shows how the assumption that pretty people are more sensitive, kind, and warm is a stereotype shared by "virtually everyone—men and women, young and old." That nobody escapes that assumption is *interesting*—it's news, something we may not have been aware of.

Illustration is painting a verbal picture using concrete details that exemplify the point being made. Illustration and explanation go hand in glove, the one being the "showing," the other the "telling." Narratives, facts, anecdotes, anything that can follow the phrase "For example . . ." helps to fill out the picture.

A well-illustrated essay is much easier to follow than one that grinds along at the level of one abstraction after another. Bridgwater's descriptions of specific experiments add both authority and detail to what would otherwise come as a banal observation: "After all, in the end it's the total human being that counts in the best relationships in our lives." Who could possibly deny that? It's why and how you get to that conclusion that counts.

Argumentation concerns the reasons, the justification, for the position you have taken, including the illustrations and other evidence. Mainly, argumentation is a matter of the reasons why and the reasons why not—the arguments pro and con. (See Chapter 4.) Argumentation is also reasoning in the sense of drawing inferences from prior statements. Bridgwater gives us an example of such inference in paragraph 7 where she says, "What this means is . . ." She does not merely summarize the contents of paragraph 6, she infers the *further conclusion* that most of us get to be "beautiful" some of the time.

In a following chapter we shall have much to say about reasoning and inference, but for now suffice to say that it is easier to argue a case after it has been adequately elaborated and illustrated. In other words, be sure to make it clear to the reader where you stand before striking out in new directions.

MAKING CONNECTIONS

A crucial aspect of establishing common ground is making connections. From the standpoint of the sheer readability of your essay, the flow of the prose, nothing is more important than making coherent connections between ideas and between paragraphs. Ironically, making sure that the separate parts of your essay are connected up is one of the commonest oversights of fledgling writers and one of the easiest to remedy. The thing to remember is that *making connections is making transitions*.

A simple and direct way to learn how to use connectors is to observe them at work in an actual essay. We have highlighted most of the connecting terms and phrases in the text of Bridgwater's essay reproduced above (pp. 43–45). Compare the highlighted terms with the full text, keeping in mind the following questions: How do the connectors contribute to the fluency and conversational tone of the essay? How, specifically, do they tie one thought to another? And, where do they most frequently occur?

Connectors signal what is going to happen, when it has begun, and when it is finished. Mostly, they indicate what the next idea is going to be: an exception (*but, alas, however*), an illustration (*for instance, for example*), a conclusion (*thus, so, therefore*), a comparison (*similarly, by contrast*), a caution (*before you decide, but it depends*), a qualification (*yet, still*), an additional item (*moreover, furthermore*), and so on.

Connectors contribute to the fluency and tone of the text by creating an atmosphere of dialogue and discussion while also keeping the reader oriented to what's going on. Accordingly, they occur most commonly at the beginnings of paragraphs and somewhere toward the middle where the qualifications, exceptions, examples, and comparisons are most likely to occur. More than that, connectors express *thoughts*—connecting thoughts like those illustrated in the preceding paragraph. Think of them as the mortar of your text without which the prose is very likely to fall to pieces.

Henceforth in your reading, make note of the author's connecting phrases (or lack of them), especially those you might find useful or could improve upon. Next to being right, using connectors well is the best thing you can do for your prose.

WRITING THE CONCLUSION

If the introduction should introduce, the conclusion should conclude; and that means more than just stopping. The two most common errors are stopping without concluding and not stopping at all. In the one instance, the writer breaks off without a summary wrap-up or statement of the main result reached in the course of the discussion. In the other instance, the writer rambles on and on, gradually running out of energy and anything to say. Not knowing how or when to stop is as much a liability in writing as elsewhere.

The importance of a proper conclusion, like a proper introduction, cannot be overestimated. First and last impressions have a way of lingering in the mind. The conclusion is both your parting shot and leave-taking; and like any departure, it can either enhance or detract from the visit.

Look again at Figure 1 (p. 47). Payne describes the classic essay conclusion as beginning narrowly and ending broadly, just the opposite of the introduction. As the diagram suggests, the conclusion inverts the order of the introduction by starting with the thesis, widening out via brief references to the body of the text, and finishing with an all-encompassing statement, the "clincher." Normally, a single paragraph will suffice to do all this.

Three elements, then, make up the conclusion:

A. A restatement of the thesis;
B. Summary allusions to the body of the text; and
C. A leading (general) final remark.

Can you identify these elements in Bridgwater's concluding paragraph? Actually, she inverts items A and B, beginning not with the thesis restatement but with allusions to the body arguments. Her summary reference to the body of the essay comes in the first sentence of paragraph 9: "Keep in mind, too, that the psychologists doing all this experimenting have focused primarily on how attractiveness affects first impressions in brief social encounters." Then comes her restatement of the thesis: "Whatever edge the beautiful have, therefore, may be evened out over time." And finally the leading, general observation: "After all, in the end it's the total human being that counts in the best relationships in our lives."

Note that the thesis restatement is a *rephrasing, not a mere repetition.* The new version should add something to our knowledge coming at the end of the discussion. Note too that Bridgwater's restatement is preceded by the illuminating connector "Whatever edge the beautiful have . . ." That phrase indicates that this *is* the beginning of the end while tying the reappearance of the thesis to the preceding paragraph. Certainly, the primary reason for restating the thesis at the end is to remind the reader of what you set out to do, now that you've done it.

The purpose of summary allusions to the body of the text is to strike resonances in the reader's mind of the main ideas developed en route. Again, making connections. This is easily accomplished by hooking in a few key words from the body. Bridgwater does it by *adding the new fact* that the experiments described in the body tended to focus on brief encounters. We never cease to be informed, even at this late stage.

The function of the last leading statement is to leave the reader with a suggestive idea that simultaneously captures the larger context of the discussion while provoking further reflection. Bridgwater does it with what amounts to a cliché, but one that has by now been carefully examined. Nowhere in an essay are you more "onstage" than here. With your exit line, you invite the reader to think on, to consider the significance of your words, to weigh their implications. Like Rhett Butler ("Frankly, my dear, I don't give a damn"), you get the last word, though seldom with such delicious finality.

PART II

THINKING FOR WRITING

CHAPTER 4

Making Sense: Reasoning for Discovery

INTRODUCTION

This chapter and the following two are placed here as strategic guides to two problems that perplex even experienced writers; namely, reasoning or argumentation and correct English usage. Both problems are obviously crucial to the writing process. Because discursive writing is a form of reasoning, the best-laid plans and ideas will fail if obscurely or awkwardly expressed. So, the more you know about reasoning and writing straight, the more you have to write *with*.

You will want to consult these three chapters more frequently as you master the procedures outlined in Part I for getting your thoughts down on paper. The right way to use them is to familiarize yourself with their contents selectively, as the need arises, as additional resources to thinking well in writing. Try to integrate them into the procedures described in Part I more and more, over time and many different topics. *The wrong way to use them is to try to absorb their contents before starting to write.*

Some of the content of these chapters is built into the earlier chapters in ways that apply directly to writing as a generative and critical activity. It is hardly necessary to master either logic or grammar as separate subjects in order to write well. Moreover, the patterns of reasoning and of expression appropriate to a particular subject or field tend to be inherent in them and best learned by exposure and example. Still, certain basics are universal; so, if you have trouble structuring your ideas logically or writing grammatically, the next three chapters will enable you better to write your mind.

HOW DO WE MAKE SENSE?

We all want to make sense of the world and of our experience. What is it? we ask. What happened? What caused it? What shall I (they) do? What do I (they) feel? Such questions constantly assail us in every aspect of our lives. However, the mere *wish* to make sense of things, by itself, implies no standards of reasoning or of evidence. The desire to understand is all too often satisfied by whim, preconception, or prejudice. Here, on the other hand, we are concerned with the kind of reasoning that is open to scrutiny and criticism and rests upon sound arguments and evidence. That kind of reasoning is the very idea and ideal of learning in any domain.

Making sense begins with questions like those above, with "hunches" about how things work or what they are, with imperatives about what one should or should not do. These lead to assertions, denials, explanations, refutations, evaluations, proposals, attitudes, and obligations. These are some of the elements of our reasoning about virtually anything. Normally, past habits of thought and action are enough to guide us through most situations. Reasoning comes into play whenever we encounter something new, unfamiliar, obstructive, or otherwise a "problem." When habits break down, the alternatives are reason or panic.

Given a problem, an unanswered question, a troublesome situation, how *do* we reason about it? Mostly we go about it in question-and-answer fashion in roughly four phases:

1. By asserting or querying what we *think* about an issue, including what it *means* to us—what we *believe* about it, how we *feel* toward it, and so on;
2. By *challenging* our own thinking, questioning our version of the matter, our information, beliefs, attitudes;
3. By challenging *other people's* versions, including their beliefs, explanations, attitudes, and what we might imagine them to think;
4. By responding to our own and others' opinions in a *series* of queries and replies.

Whether we do this silently, aloud, or in writing, and whether we go through all four phases, reasoning itself tends to proceed in this way from "hunches and first thoughts" to "reservations and misgivings" to "questions and challenges to others" to "replies to the objections." Often these phases will overlap or be repeated.

When one is struggling with a difficult problem, the typical result is a series of statements pro and con: "on the one hand this . . . but on the other hand that . . ." leading to a conclusion. Normally, this is how we assess facts and events, try to explain them, make plans, concoct plausible alternatives, note the evidence for or against our views, probe the opinions of others, and take account of possible objections. Other names, besides *reasoning,* for this kind of mental activity are *critical thinking* and *rational inquiry.* We prefer *reasoning for discovery.* By whatever name, it is thinking directed toward the assessment and evaluation of things, and it can be done well or badly.

Two features of reasoning as a personal experience deserve mention here as well. First is the fact that reasoning is less a matter of being *given* anything than of *taking a point of view,* of reaching out through search and discovery. Second is the fact that reasoning is both generative and critical (like writing); it is as much a matter of discovering new ideas as of scrutinizing and testing them.

Let us briefly look at some results of recent research into the nature of reasoning—the process by which we make sense of things.

REASONING AS PROBING

Experimental research on reasoning led by D. N. Perkins of the Harvard Graduate School of Education suggests that the competent reasoner proceeds by *challenging and altering* his or her premises while thinking through a problem; that is, by accumulating then abandoning assumptions generated in the course of live inquiry. Perkins cites the following example of "everyday reasoning" directed to the question "Would a law requiring a five-cent deposit on bottles and cans reduce litter?"

> The law wants people to return the bottles for five cents, instead of littering them. But I don't think five cents is enough nowadays to get people to bother. But wait, it isn't just five cents at a blow, because people can accumulate cases of bottles or bags of cans in their basements and take them back all at once, so probably they would do that. Still, those probably aren't the bottles and cans that get littered anyway; it's the people out on picnics or kids hanging around the streets and parks that litter bottles and cans, and they sure wouldn't bother to return them for a nickel. But someone else might— boy scout and girl scout troops and other community organizations very likely would collect the bottles and cans as a combined community service and fund-raising venture; I know they do that sort of thing. So litter would be reduced. [Perkins et al., 1983, p. 178]

Besides illustrating everyday reasoning, the quoted passage is also a splendid example of thinking in writing; it shows well how the two converge in one activity. Ignore for now whether you agree or disagree with the conclusion. Attend instead to how it was reached. Note that each sentence challenges the one preceding in a series pro and con. The effect is not only to advance the argument to its conclusion but to proliferate alternative construals of the situation and the reasons for or against them.

This is much simpler and more direct than trying to apply abstract rules of deductive or inductive logic. Formal principles of logic are of course implicit in everyday reasoning, but like grammatical rules, it isn't necessary to know them to use them. As Perkins says, "Effective reasoning . . . depends on an active effort to interrogate one's knowledge base in order to construct arguments pro and con" (p. 186). "In contrast with reasoning as classically conceived, premises change and accumulate as the argument proceeds rather than being given at the outset. Second, the premises are somewhat constructive, elaborating the reasoner's understanding of the situation rather than merely objecting" (p. 178).

Perkins's second point is particularly insightful in distinguishing nit-picking and baleful naysaying from *constructive* criticism rooted in curiosity and a drive to understand and to assess matters carefully.

How does this bear upon writing reasonably and logically? Most of the writing we do, even technical writing, is structured around the leading questions, objections, and counterreplies that we (the writers) or they (the readers) are likely to have. That holds true even where graphs, statistics, formal proofs, or special techniques like cost-benefit analysis are involved.

What this means is that reasoning *and* writing in the service of live inquiry reaches beyond anything given—to discovery. Or, to put it another way, *reasoning creates more knowledge than it is given.* However, a common assumption of logic texts and not a few writing manuals is that reasoning mainly consists of testing the validity, probability, and truth of conclusions already reached. Such a reduction of reasoning to logic and procedures of verification overlooks its primary function, *to probe into the unknown.* In other words, reasoning is inquiry and discovery as well as validation and verification. Like writing, reasoning too has two sides, only one of which gets the lion's share of attention.

Typically, we think and converse in what logicians call *enthymemes*—truncated argument forms in which one or several premises, perhaps the conclusion itself, are suppressed or taken for granted. For instance, "That's theft!" uttered by the prosecution in a courtroom will usually be clear enough without adding the major premise ("Acts of theft are wrong and illegal") or the conclusion ("Therefore, that's wrong and illegal"). The point is that *reasoning uses logic inventively* to solve problems.

Looked at from a problem-solving point of view, the major stimuli to inventive reasoning are the three questions: *What?, Why?,* and *Why not?* They take different forms: What exactly is the issue here? What am I trying to say? What is their proposal? Why is this idea, this explanation, this proposal a good one? And conversely, why is this idea a bad one? Why will this plan fail?

What?, Why?, and Why not? lie at the core of everyday reasoning. To competent thinkers in every domain they become second nature, driving first thoughts on through objections and challenges to a conclusion. They propel us out of complacency to solve problems and to devise better plans of action. Repeated over and over again, in hundreds of situations, they enable us to come up with the best ideas possible, which means the most plausible ideas imaginable.

PLAUSIBILITY

Plausibility, meaning literally "deserving of applause" from the Latin *plaudere,* concerns the believability or credibility of ideas. Credibility in turn is a matter of survival; that is, of ideas surviving severe tests aimed at falsifying them. *The tougher the test, the greater the credibility.* That is how scientific experimentation and ordinary experience alike work to refine and to revise our well-hatched if sometimes half-cocked notions and plans. This is the other side of reasoning, the side that has to do with putting new ideas to the tests of logic and observation (see Karl Popper, 1968). Reasoning aims not only at concocting plausible new ideas but at deciding which among them is most plausible, credible, believable.

Belief is not an all-or-nothing thing. It admits of degrees, as shown by such common remarks as "I'm sure of that," "moderately sure," "unsure," "doubtful," and so on. Moreover, the line separating what *seems* plausible from what *is* plausible, between conjecture and supported opinion, is often very fine and fluctuating. Our only defense against fancy, prejudice, and deception is the ability to query the credentials of candidates for our credence. Again, What?, Why?, and Why not?

We hold beliefs with varying degrees of confidence according to the evidence supporting them; that is, if we wish to be rational about what we believe (Nickerson, 1982, p. 47). We weigh the available evidence, or, lacking direct access, the credibility of the source. For example, the announcement of impending victory by a campaigning politician elicits less confidence than the same announcement by an independent pollster.

That raises another point about rationally held beliefs; namely, that they may be strengthened, modified, or dropped—the degree of their plausibility changing as new information becomes available. We may even suspend judgment where the evidence is inconclusive, in a measured agnosticism, as it were, of the sort that is reflex among scientific investigators. Under normal circumstances, we rely upon evidence as a measure of the plausibility of the beliefs held rather than the personal forcefulness or conviction of the believer.

Finally, plausibility is different from persuasiveness. What persuades us often goes beyond evidence to appeals to emotion, desire, habit, preconception, or prejudice. The most rational among us is susceptible to irrational appeal on some matters. Nor would we have it otherwise where personal preference and taste are concerned. We like what we like, but it can be dangerous to believe what we like. The plausibility of our beliefs depends upon the reasons and evidence that can be marshaled to support them. By definition, *rational* persuasion is logical, but persuasion is not always rational. We trust that you want to be rational about what you believe and about what you ask others to believe. Accordingly, we will now talk about generating plausible ideas.

The rest of this chapter outlines some practical strategies for making your message both sound and persuasive. We will show you how better to organize and use the tools of reasoning that are already second nature to you. In the following chapter, you will learn how to assess the raw materials of the reasoning process; and, finally, how to present your arguments in the most persuasive ways. But remember: This is background information and advice to be absorbed gradually. Use it as you need it, incorporating more and more of it into your personal habits of thought.

REASONING BY QUESTIONING

The tools of reasoning described below are mostly familiar to you as habits of thought that may never have surfaced to consciousness in any systematic way. The objective here is to enable you to take control and make better use of the reasoning equipment already in your possession.

Recall the three mental prods to inventiveness: What?, Why?, and Why not? The first step toward clear thinking is to clarify to yourself exactly what you think and why. Those questions take many forms and apply as much to what you read as to what you think and write. For example, it is a useful strategy when reading or listening to ask yourself, What in essence is the author (or speaker) saying here? How in a single sentence would I summarize the gist of it? "The author thinks _____ because _____." The phrase preceding the "because" is *what* the author thinks; the phrase after contains the reasons *why*. Clearly, these are not the same questions when asked of oneself and when asked of others; and just as clearly, pursuit of the question Why not? must follow answers to the questions What? and Why? That is the governing sequence to keep in mind.

Let us now divide the basic sequence into a subordinate series of checklist questions covering the main routes that reasoning for problem solving takes.

What?

The "what" of the matter can be most anything. When you are thinking, reading, or writing on demand, it is convenient to think of the question What? as having three focuses:

- Problems
- Methods
- Solutions

When you read or reflect upon an issue, ask yourself, What exactly is the problem here? What is the (best) method for solving it? What is the (best) solution? The word *problem* is deliberately vague, referring to "the main issue," "the question," "the trouble," and so forth. The word *best* in parentheses reflects the differences between a method that *is* used and one that you think *ought* to be used, and a solution proffered versus one you think actually solves the problem. Naturally, they will not always be the same unless you believe everything you read!

Where the question is one of establishing policy or a course of action, the What? subheadings will vary somewhat. For example: problems, methods, solutions, policy; or proposals, benefits, procedures, and so on. The nature of the material will usually indicate clearly enough what's What? The underlying idea is always the same: What is going on here? What is the issue? The approach taken? The outcomes, the recommendations, the results?

The problems/methods/solutions breakdown of the question What? functions also to guide your thinking when matters are maddeningly confusing. Thinking "problems, methods, solutions" will steer your mind toward a clearer *orientation* on the problem at hand with increasing *specification* of the relevant details. Which brings us to the question Why?

Why?

The question Why? concerns the "because" clause in "I (they) think _____ because _____." The key words here are:

- Reasons
- Evidence
- Arguments

Don't worry about the fact that these are frequently overlapping concepts; just keep them in mind as catch phrases to focus your thinking on whatever *supports* (or is supposed to support) the position described on the left-hand side of the "because" clause. At this point, you are ferreting out the case *pro* the position taken.

For example, it is a *reason* (motive, justification) for carrying an umbrella that it might rain. The fact that profits are rising is *evidence* that the new management policies are working. It is an *argument* for fiscal restraint that if we do not reduce the national debt, the nation will plunge into a recession.

You are in no position to criticize until it is clear *what* the position taken is and *why* it is held. To that end, it is an extremely useful exercise to set down in writing the reasons why such and such is, or seems, or is held, to be the case. The objective here is further *specification* and *clarification* of the position taken. Once that is done, you are primed to mount objections or to counter objections that may refute, alter, or even support the position originally taken. That brings us to the question Why not?

Why Not?
So far, you have been in quest of what you (or someone else) think and why. What? and Why? show the power of positive thinking, but there is a positive power to negative thinking as well called constructive criticism. That is where the question Why not? comes in. As mentioned earlier, ideas increase their credibility by surviving tough tests. *Reasoning that is both inventive and sound requires that you be able to challenge your own ideas—your own What? and Why?— as well as anticipate the challenges of others. In other words, Why not?*

Certainly not all the writing you do will take the argument form of thesis and defense. A simple narrative or survey description of events or illustration may not require an argument. But where you need to reason, to weigh and assess ideas and evidence pro and con, the argument form is your best defense. It provides a strong framework for a large percentage of academic, technical, and business writing where it is required to make a case for something. And the core of making a case is being able to anticipate and to articulate Why not?

Drawing upon D. N. Perkins's investigations of everyday reasoning, following are the nine most common ways of asking Why not?, arranged in the order of their frequency.* If some seem obvious and familiar, they are; indeed, all are quite common. We have given each of them a descriptive name and a schematized formulation to make them easier to remember. Familiarize yourself with them to the point where you can use them and recognize when others are using them.

Challenge to Definitions and Terms. A very common objection or reason why not is to query the meanings attached to the crucial words involved in an assertion or inference. For example: "Wage and price controls are fundamentally incompatible with the free-enterprise system." Objection: "But what do you mean by a 'free-enterprise system'?" Or again: "Rembrandt is an artist; Jackson Pollack is not an artist." Such a blanket judgment invites the reply: "But how would you define 'artist'?" Or "Real men don't eat quiche." "Oh? What is a 'real man'?" The scheme for this type of objection is: *If A then B. No, that depends on what you mean by A (or by B).*

---

*Perkins identified fifty-five categories of objections (reasons why not) including a long list of those frequently rehearsed in the logic textbooks: contradiction, question begging, equivocation, counterexample, neglected distinction, reduction to absurdity, hasty generalization, biased sample, and so on (p. 181). Of the total fifty-five categories, however, only eight (those listed below, following "Challenge to Definitions and Terms") accounted for 80 percent of objections commonly raised, each of the eight categories accounting for from 5 percent to 20 percent of objections raised in ordinary reasoning situations of the sort illustrated by the bottle bill narrative (p. 68). Being mainly interested in scientific description, Perkins is careful to note that the eight most common objections are "constructs of the experimenters designed to sort a body of data, constructs that have no necessary reality as guiding schemata in the minds of skilled reasoners" (p. 183). Our concern, by contrast, is with how best to put such constructs to practical use.

Different Conclusion or Effect. Beginning with the same situation or set of facts as the opposing position, one reasons to a different conclusion. For example, the shop manager might argue, "If the company adopted a policy of strict time accounting, worker efficiency would be increased, and, hence, productivity too." To which the floor steward might reply, "If the company adopted a policy of strict time accounting, workers would become resentful, less efficient, and hence, productivity would be decreased." The result is no mere alteration of the original argument, but an entirely different interpretation of the same situation. The scheme: *If A then B. No, if A then not B but C instead.*

Different Antecedent or Cause. Here the reason why not is that the presumed antecedent of the argument fails to account for the consequent, which is actually due to something else. In other words, there is agreement on the effect, but disagreement on its cause. An argument from effect to cause might look like this: "Academic standards in the public schools are declining, because the teachers themselves aren't educated." Objection: "There are many other causes of academic decline such as deteriorating social conditions, parental indifference, and the like." Or, arguing from cause to effect: "Marketing efficiency is the reason why profits are up this month." "No, simple increased demand and our company being the nearest source for the product are the reasons why profits are up this month." The scheme: *A causes B. No (not necessarily), C or D causes (or could cause) B. Or, B is the effect of A. No, B is the effect of C.*

Interference. The objection here is that an intervening factor short-circuits the inference, which otherwise might hold. For example: "Ours will be a better society if our first concern is justice, not national defense." To which it might be objected: "Formerly, that was true, but nuclear weapons have made that an outmoded argument. The threat of nuclear extinction requires putting defense first." Interference is a close cousin of "Different Conclusion or Effect" above, but attributes the different scenario to an external, intervening factor overlooked in the original argument. The scheme: *If A then B. Normally, perhaps, but because of C, B does not follow from A.*

Irrelevant Reasons. People often argue to a conclusion on grounds that have little or nothing to do with the conclusion or bear only weakly upon it. For instance: "The poor will always be with us, so there's no justification for social welfare." Objection: "The fact, if it is a fact, that the poor will always be with us does not imply an absence of justification for social welfare." And carrying the objection further: "That could well be the principal reason *for* social welfare." Another example: "That film contains nudity and foul language, and, therefore, is worthless and immoral." Objection: "Nudity and swearing in and of themselves imply neither artistic worthlessness nor immorality." The scheme: *A implies B (or, B because of A). No, A has little or no bearing on B.*

Too Much/Too Little. In arguments referring to causal factors, especially where motives are involved, the objection often arises that there is too much or too little of something for the consequent to follow. For instance, in the bottle bill narrative (p. 68), the first objection to the presumed effects of the bill is "I don't think five cents is enough nowadays to get people to bother." And for an example of too much: To the claim that "harsher punishment is required to restore order in unruly classrooms," it might be replied that "harsher treatment provokes stronger resistance." The scheme: *If A then B. No, A is too much (too little) to bring about B.*

Factor Ignored. This objection says that the inference, assertion, or explanation put forth ignores a critical subclass or factor involved in the particular situation at hand. For instance, it might be argued: "The best way to ensure high educational standards would be to impose uniform curricula and tests." A likely objection: "The remedy proposed overlooks the different needs and interests of large groups of students." This objection is also illustrated in the bottle bill narrative, where the reasoner distinguishes between those who consume beverages at home and those out on the streets or on picnics who are mostly responsible for the litter. The scheme: *If A then B. No, the argument ignores factor C; therefore, not B.*

Counterexample. Here the claim is that the situation *in fact* differs from that supposed in the argument. Example: "Punishment, threats, and, in general, 'the whip' are the most effective controls of human behavior." Counterexample: "In experimental fact, positive incentives and rewards are both more effective and longer-lasting ways of changing behavior." Counterexamples are particularly powerful reasons why not, because they are facts, not *predictions,* for example, that the effects will be thus and so, or that people will react this way or that. Counterexamples are findings—actual facts-to-the-contrary that stop an argument cold in its tracks. The scheme: *A's are always B's. No, here is an A that is not B. Or, A causes B. No, this B occurs quite independently of A.*

Saving Revision. This reason why not calls for an alteration in the original argument to fend off an objection; in effect, a saving reply to an objection or reason why not. For example, to the objection that proximity and increased demand, rather than marketing efficiency, account for increased profits, it might be replied, "Yes, but other companies are equally accessible, and marketing explains why potential buyers chose our company rather than the others." Or, to return to the bottle bill, to the complaint that five cents is too little incentive, it might be answered, "Probably not by itself. But a bottle bill and the associated publicity will make people more environmentally conscious, so they will be more careful about litter." The scheme: *A does not imply B. No, combined with (or taking account of) C, A does imply B.*

The latter reason why not brings us full circle to a reply to the objections, or what amounts to a defense of the original claim.

A leading feature of these most common challenges is that "most of the objections extend the reasoner's current model of the situation being reasoned about" (Perkins et al., 1983, p. 183). That is, they tend toward elaboration of one's thinking about a particular issue. As well, they are highly content-specific and directed at questions that the available information (or lack of it) raises. Again, reasoning is probing, and the questions What?, Why?, and Why not? in their various forms reflect the well-honed, habitual responses of the competent reasoner. Together they are a powerful force for generating the raw materials for writing.

INDUCTION AND DEDUCTION

This is a good place to describe the connections between the methods of reasoning outlined above and the logical functions of deduction and induction. Whatever practical reasoning strategies one adopts, reasoning itself, as a logical process, goes in either or both of two directions: inward from the welter of facts at the periphery to a common core of general statements or principles, or outward from general principles or assumptions to particular facts or classes of facts. The one is called induction, from the Latin *inducere* meaning "to lead in," and the other deduction, from *deducere* meaning "to lead out or away." Both are forms of *inference* or ways of supporting a proposition or set of propositions by others in an argument.

Induction is the ability to detect regularities in events and to generalize from particular instances. For example, by observing large numbers of trees one might discover that larches or tamaracks, unlike most conifers, are deciduous (shed their needles annually). Knowing this, or taking it on authority, one may deduce that not all conifers are "evergreens"; or that Jones's claim to have only evergreens on his woodlot is contradicted by the fact that a large tamarack stands in the middle of it. Deduction, then, is the ability to detect what is consistent or inconsistent with one's assumptions: what does or does not follow from them.

You need only examine the propositions asserted or assumed to determine what can or cannot be deduced from them separately or together. Whereas, to induce a (reliable) generalization to the effect that personal contacts are more effective than résumés in securing executive jobs, one would have to search the job histories of many executives in many businesses for the evidence. The scourge of deduction is inconsistency (or contradiction); the scourge of induction is lack of evidence or too little of it. (See Appendix A for a more detailed account.)

As the preceding examples show, induction and deduction are joined in nearly all arguments—if not always reliably or validly. (See Appendix A on probability and the difference between validity and truth.) Much of what we call commonsense reasoning, of the sort represented by the methods of reasoning above, is the combined inductive and deductive wisdom of everyday experience. Such experience yields a wealth of general observations about life and the world from which we are liable to reason deductively with rather too much haste at times. The result is common nonsense rather than the wisdom of experience. That is why we need to carefully guide the reasoning process by questioning ourselves and others.

Not uncommonly do people reason like this: "No one should object to a loyalty oath except those who have something to hide." The statement assumes that only those guilty of disloyalty object to loyalty oaths—that no other grounds for objecting exist—a very hasty assumption indeed. (The objection, incidentally, is "factor ignored.") The inductive grounds of our everyday reasoning are frequently concealed in implied (unstated) assumptions based on inadequate evidence. Dragged into the open, such assumptions will often crumble instantly for lack of any adequate support.

The best way to absorb any set of skills or routines is to use them. Practice the reasoning strategies outlined above by keeping them in mind checklist fashion as you deliberate about everyday matters and decisions, such as, Shall I take that holiday this month or next? What can be done to increase sales without adding personnel? What are my career options under the company's new five-year plan? The idea is to monitor your actual reasoning processes in order to increase their efficiency. To make that easier, we have provided a Reasoning Checklist at the end of this chapter. You may find it convenient at first to keep a few photocopies of the list handy.

Certainly there is more to reasoning psychologically and logically than we have presented here. The tools of reasoning are merely a beginning in common sense for guiding your thinking and organizing the results. *They enable you to choose and to check your arguments first and then to write them up.*

You are now ready to compose—to organize your ideas topically and sequentially, as earlier described in Chapters 2 and 3, and also as described in the next chapter on reasoning for presentation.

Using the tools of reasoning this way will help you to focus your thinking and to anticipate objections. As well, they will help you to increase your understanding of the topic in question and to organize that understanding for presentation to others. In effect, you will learn how to *get* your case and then to *make* it.

REASONING CHECKLIST

What?

1. What is your problem (question, topic)?

_____

_____

(If more than one, list them succinctly or make out a separate sheet for each problem.)
    2. How do you plan to investigate the problem?

_____

_____

(Fact-finding, experiment, interpretation, evaluation?)
    3. What is your solution (conclusion, thesis, recommendation)?

_____

_____

(State the "bottom line" as briefly as possible.)

Why?
    1. What reasons (objectives, motives, justifications) support your solution to the problem?

_____

_____

    2. What evidence (facts, data, findings) support your solution?

_____

_____

    3. What arguments (principles, values, explanations) support your solution?

_____

_____

(Note your pro arguments in a word or two.)

Why Not?
    Go through the list of reasons why not, checking each one to see whether an objection of that sort can be raised to your statement of the problem, your methods, or your conclusions. Then consider whether any of your reasons why are similarly vulnerable.

1. Challenge to definitions and terms

_____

2. Different conclusion or effect

_____

3. Different antecedent or cause

_____

4. Interference

_____

5. Irrelevant reasons

_____

6. Too much/too little

_____

7. Factor ignored

_____

8. Counterexample

_____

9. Saving revision

_____

CHAPTER 5

Writing Sense: Reasoning for Presentation

ANALYZING REASONING'S RAW MATERIALS

Having collected your arguments, objections, and counter-replies, the next task is to sort them according to criteria that will enhance their presentation. The criteria will of course vary with the nature of the material and the intended audience, but four criteria for sorting arguments are universal. They are:

- Thesis versus antithesis
- Arguments pro versus arguments con
- Strong arguments versus weak arguments
- Persuasive versus unpersuasive arguments

Thesis Versus Antithesis

A thesis is an assertion supportable by arguments. An antithesis is a directly opposing or contrasting assertion. Some opposing claims are *contradictory:* Only one of the two claims could be true. "All bosses are brutes" versus "My boss is not a brute," or "Not all bosses are brutes." Other opposing claims are *contrary,* a weaker form of opposition: Both claims could be true but not both false, or both claims could be false but not both true. For instance, "Some bosses are brutes" versus "Some bosses are not brutes" could both be true but not both false. Or "All bosses are brutes" versus "All bosses are saints" could both be false but not both true.* The details of logical opposition need not detain us here. For present purposes, it is sufficient to be able to recognize and to articulate your own position on an issue plus the opposing position. For instance, if it is your opinion that "the company should *not* purchase more computer equipment, because . . ." then the antithesis is "The company *should* purchase more computer equipment, because . . ."

There are three reasons why it is important to articulate the opposing view as well as your own. First, it helps you to clarify your own position by contrast; second, it enables you to anticipate objections to your views; and third, it enables you to use the opposition in the presentation of your own case; e.g., "Some think . . . because . . . but in fact . . ."

Arguments Pro Versus Arguments Con

Arguments pro are whatever reasons support your thesis, whereas arguments con are whatever reasons count against it. For example, a reason favoring the view that the company should not purchase more computer equipment is the fact that profits are insufficient to make such a large capital investment. A reason counting against that opinion might be that new computer equipment has the potential for greatly increasing profits.

Where the opposition between competing views is sharp

---

*The array of relations between contradictory and contrary statements is traditionally called the Square of Opposition, because they are usually represented on a square. For a good account of these and related topics, see Irving M. Copi's *Introduction to Logic,* 6th ed. (New York: Macmillan, 1982). Another useful companion to the present discussion is Monroe C. Beardsley's *Thinking Straight: Principles of Reasoning for Readers and Writers,* 4th ed. (Englewood Cliffs, N.J.: Prentice-Hall, 1975).

and clear, the arguments supporting the one position will usually count directly or indirectly against the other. Still other reasons may cut against both positions; for example, if the company is contemplating new production techniques, it makes sense to defer any decision about new computers until the needs of the company are clearer.

Strong Versus Weak Arguments

The relative strength or weakness of arguments depends upon their credibility, which in turn depends upon the severity of the challenges to them. For instance, "Profits are too low" is a much stronger argument against purchasing new computer equipment than "We are not sure that the available equipment meets our needs." (Consultation with the computer companies would readily remove that obstacle.) The "profits are too low" argument is somewhat weakened, however, if management declares, "The company is prepared to take any reasonable risk to increase profits." And taking the counterargument one step further, if someone announces, "A cheap computer system, well within present profit margins, exists that can meet any projected needs of the company," that information totally eclipses (by counterexample) the "profits are too low" argument.

There are no hard-and-fast rules for assessing the relative strength or weakness of arguments apart from the particular circumstances in which they occur. Common sense and experience with a particular subject matter are often the best guides. As in the example above, arguments will change in their relative strength or weakness depending upon how much is known at the moment and the inflow of new information.

Because most situations in which we are called upon to make a case for something are changeable, we recommend that you perform a "situational analysis" once your main arguments and replies to counterarguments are in hand. That means making a rough estimate of which of them count most heavily in your favor, and which the least, *in those circumstances.* Admittedly, this is a kind of guesswork compounded of many factors going beyond the sheer logical strength of your case. But assuming a *rational audience,* and setting aside emotional, political, or other "irrational" factors, try rating your arguments on a scale of 1 to 4 as follows:

1. Very strong
2. Strong
3. Moderate
4. Weak

However crude, this will give you some estimate of the logical strength of your case, assuming people are rational and willing to listen. (You will recall that this is a critical factor in writing the body of an essay.) The ideal situation is to have a veritable army of very strong arguments supporting your position, but that seldom happens. More likely, you will find differences of strength among your arguments with most of them falling into the moderate to strong categories (that's what makes controversial matters controversial). Just remember that there are three sides to every story: your side, the other person's side, and the truth. Your objective is to make your side look more like the truth.

Persuasive Versus Unpersuasive Arguments

Having assessed your arguments rationally, now you can assess their emotional appeal. Persuasiveness concerns the relative impact on a given audience of your arguments. If relative *strength* concerns the logical force of your case assuming the complete rationality of your audience, relative *impact* concerns the projected effects of your case on an audience that is not completely rational. Judgments of relative impact are even more "situational" than those of relative strength, because they sweep in the audience's interests, values, biases, and possible responses. A third party can impartially assess your logic and the strength of your arguments, but only your audience will judge the *significance* of what you have to say (though you must take care to try to estimate that significance).

Take the simple statement "It's raining!" Imagine the difference in impact of that statement uttered to drought-ravaged farmers, to flood-threatened home owners, or to phlegmatic Englishmen in November. True or false, the statement's impact varies widely with the audience. In other words, impact reaches beyond logic and reasons to include psychology and emotions.

Estimates of impact involve rational and emotional considerations together: assessments of what your audience is likely to find convincing, persuasive, offensive, threatening; assessments of your aims and expectations compared to theirs; assessments of how best to present your case given your purposes and their anticipated responses; assessments of how best to neutralize or diminish their negative reactions and to capitalize on their positive reactions; and so on. Remembering the rational strengths of your arguments, review them again on the following scale:

1. Very persuasive
2. Strongly persuasive
3. Moderately persuasive
4. Unpersuasive

Except where reactions are highly predictable, such as "War is inevitable!" shouted at a pacifist convention, estimates of impact tend to be probing and "psychological," centering on the question "How will they react to this?" Repeat this question over and over as you review your ideas. It touches not only on the specific points to be made but on the language and style of their presentation, their order, and persuasiveness. For that is the objective of your reasoning now: persuasion; and persuasion is an art.

To help you to acquire the art of persuasion, use the Impact Checklist below to estimate the appeal that your case and supporting arguments are likely to have on a specific audience. As you practice using the Impact Checklist, keep in mind the relations between reasoning and persuading described in the next section.

IMPACT CHECKLIST

To sort your ideas for their impact, focus the question "How will they react to this?" on the following:

1. How are they likely to react to my overall case?

_____

_____

(Briefly describe the anticipated response.)

2. Which of the arguments *supporting* my case are they likely to find most convincing, most compelling, least offensive?

_____

_____

(List them by quick reference.)

3. Which of the arguments *against* my case are they likely to find most convincing, compelling, attractive?

_____

_____

(List them by quick reference.)

4. How can I present my replies to their anticipated objections in ways that are convincing *and* acceptable to them?

_____

_____

_____

(Think here of attitude, tone, keeping their attention.)

REASONING AND PERSUADING

Order, tact, timing, poise, and courtesy are as important to effective communication in writing as they are in speech—especially so where persuasion is concerned. A straightforward command ("All personnel will report to Command Headquarters at 0800 hours") or statement of fact ("The student attrition rate is 5 percent for the month of January") makes no attempt to convince. "Orders is orders" and "Facts is facts," as the sayings go, but facts also invite interpretation and explanation. It is when we begin to *argue* about things that persuasion becomes an issue.

As mentioned, reasoning and persuading are not the same, even if ideally we prefer a considerable degree of overlap. The procedures by which we arrive at a logical conclusion or proposal will not automatically produce a convincing case in speech or writing. By the same token, a highly persuasive tirade to an already "converted" audience may amount to little more than a blatant appeal to prejudice or stereotype. ("My country right or wrong!" Or "Syd Macho uses Old Sweat aftershave—shouldn't you?")

Rational persuasion lies between the extremes of pure logic and pure feeling, and for that very reason draws upon both. If your objective is to move people, to change their minds, to advocate or defend an opinion, then you must take care to orient them, to introduce them to the issue sympathetically, to draw them into your arguments and on to your conclusions in a manner that holds their attention and invites their responses.

The format of the traditional essay, you will recall, is intended to accomplish exactly that by going beyond mere narrative reporting of facts or information to argue a point. That, incidentally, marks the difference between an *essay* and an expository theme or purely factual report.

Another way of organizing reasoning's results focuses on the main *kinds of question* that drive most forms of discursive writing. This sorting is in addition to the sorting of arguments just described. It goes directly to the logical nature of the issues addressed.

THREE SORTS OF QUESTIONS

Three sorts of questions motivate inquiry and advocacy in any form: What are the facts? Why are they as they are? (What explains them?) And are the facts good or bad? Let us call these respectively:

- Factual questions
- Interpretative questions
- Evaluative questions

These are the standing questions, as it were, behind the What?, Why?, and Why not? of the reasoning process that aims to establish the facts, diagnose them, and evaluate them with some specific end or issue in view.*

The basic division is between *description* and *explanation,* on the one hand, and *evaluation* and *prescription,* on the other: between what *is* the case and what *ought to be* the case (or done about it). The very word *interpretation* is sometimes ambiguous between explaining, on the one hand, and evaluating, on the other. A few examples will suffice to show the difference, putting factual and interpretative (ex-

---

*The sharp distinction of convenience we make between facts and their interpretation (including theories and hypotheses) is untenable in epistemology, the study of knowledge. In many areas of science they draw close together, facts becoming mini-theories, as it were. Nor are values absent from scientific-theory construction, still less from scientific controversy. See, for instance, Stephen Jay Gould, *The Mismeasure of Man* (New York: Norton, 1981); also, Thomas Kuhn, *The Structure of Scientific Revolutions,* 2nd ed. (Chicago: University of Chicago Press, 1970). Again, our concern is to elaborate a series of broad distinctions and categories useful in guiding the activity of reasoning for writing.

planatory) questions in the left column and evaluative questions in the right column.

Questions of Fact and Cause	Questions of Value
How much has production declined and for how long? Is the decline due to poor management or decreased demand?	Should management be replaced or should we launch a new advertising campaign?
Are art courses the first to be eliminated from shrinking school budgets? Why is that?	Should art be a required subject in schools or eliminated altogether?
What is the assay and extent of the abestos deposits in New Brunswick? What is their geological origin?	Is the company justified in undertaking asbestos mining in New Brunswick?
Did the Riff Raff Company lie about its assets and profits to its shareholders?	Is it permissible to "strategically misrepresent" a company's assets?
What are the effects of acid rain along the Canada-U.S.A. border, and how many square miles of forest lands are affected?	Ought Canada and the U.S.A. submit to international arbitration on the acid rain issue?
Were Sacco and Vanzetti found guilty of murder?	Ought Sacco and Vanzetti to have been found guilty of murder?

Questions of fact and cause are fundamentally different from questions of value. Answers to the one sort of question will not automatically result in answers to the other sort. How things are does not necessarily determine how they ought to be, or conversely. So, in most strongly contended matters (assuming agreement on the facts), two levels of controversy predominate: What explains this? And what justifies this?

Factual and interpretative (causal) issues tend to be either-or, affirmative or negative; either something is the case or it is not. Even where the facts are uncertain (e.g., "How many tons of Allied shipping were destroyed by U-boats in World War II?"), the very asking of the question supposes that evidence exists (or once existed) that would settle the issue to anyone's satisfaction. It may never actually be settled, and the controversy may be heated, but it is at least clear what *in principle* would settle the issue. Accordingly, it is often easier to ascertain what kinds of reasons and evidence would settle a factual/causal issue than what kinds of reasons and principles would settle an evaluative issue.

Agreement on an evaluative issue presupposes consensus, agreement on certain controlling values shared by the parties concerned. They often don't. Therefore, it is quite possible to agree on the facts and to disagree on what ought to be done about them. We are not here referring to the kind of disagreement that originates in lack of information ("Should we sell our shares now or wait?") but to disagreement that originates in differences of principle. For example, questions of the morality (not the legality) of abortion, of nuclear warfare, of human rights, of sexual behavior and preference, of free speech, of the best form of government, of the aims of education, of proper professional behavior, of marital fidelity, of social welfare—none of these issues can be resolved merely by appeal to the relevant facts. Values are a crucial factor in them all.

For that reason, it is crucial to keep clear in your mind what *sort* of question you are addressing when reasoning about an issue and later too, of course, when writing up your case for presentation to others.

CONCLUSION: THE RANGE OF REASONING

Reasoning encompasses more than mastery of the special techniques of deductive or inductive logic, statistics, or econometrics. While any of these might be required for one or another kind of writing, neither reasoning generally nor reasoning for writing can be reduced to any one or combination of them.

Reasoning centers around an enormously wide range of habits, know-how, strategies, procedures, rules, and spontaneous insights—summarized as "experience" or "judgment"—used to formulate and assess beliefs. Our beliefs concern every aspect of our lives, our experience, and the world.

Harkening back to Chapter 1, reasoning is a symbolic activity not at all confined to language, as witness the variety of mathematical, diagrammatic, notational, and other forms of symbolization. For purposes of *writing,* however, reasoning is so closely language-bound as to be inseparable from it. If one fails to comprehend a statement or its implications, is that a failure of logic or of language? Conversely, if one is vague or ambiguous or contradictory in what one writes, is that a failure of language or of logic? The questions are misleading in suggesting a separation where, in fact, the precise use of language is the sine qua non alike of good sense, sound logic, and effective writing.

Writing as thinking, or more specifically as reasoning on paper, is a skill. As a skill, it can be learned and taught, and done well or badly. We cannot hope to write and reason well about everything; nor should we hastily assume that the reasoning and writing skills, say, of business will carry over to politics or conversely. Every field and discipline has its demands and standards of performance and expression culminating in a kind of "judgment" or superior insight not reducible to rules and routines however much they may be presupposed.

Such judgment has to do with what's relevant, important, dispensable, plausible, convincing, and, perhaps most crucial, *what's questionable*. Learning to express oneself well in writing is no substitute for such judgment or the experience that engenders it, but think how much more powerful such judgment becomes when it combines with the power of clear, persuasive expression—particularly for those who must write on demand.

CHAPTER 6

A User's Guide to Grammar and Punctuation

TRIM OR TECHNIQUE?

What could be duller than grammar? Such a gaggle of stuffy dos and don'ts of so-called formalized expression! What does it matter anyway if one manages to get one's message across? And if the prose needs "prettying up," why not just turn it over to a good editor or secretary?

O.K., but consider the analogous argument: What could be duller than navigation? Such a tangle of trigonometric rules of formalized space! What does it matter if one manages to get to one's destination? And if the course needs "prettying up," why not turn it over to a good map reader or deckhand?

Fine on both counts, *if* you have no difficult voyages to take or documents to write. Like navigation, grammar and punctuation are powerful aids to getting through. While no substitute for knowing where you want to go, they can assist you in avoiding hazards and maintaining a strong sense of direction.

There is no end to what you can learn about language and its varieties of written expression. Grammar and punctuation are no exceptions. As areas for study, they bear a relation to practical writing that is similar to the connection between formal logic and practical reasoning of the kind discussed in Chapters 4 and 5. It is easy to get lost in a labyrinth of distinctions and definitions. Accordingly, we prefer a bottom-up to a top-down approach, stressing what is immediately useful as contrasted with abstract rules and explanations. The latter we leave to the several excellent guides to grammar and punctuation now in print (see Appendix B). Instead, we present here the minimum you need for self-defense against the most common errors of grammar and punctuation. Beyond that, we hope to convince you that, like the basics of reasoning, the basics of grammar and punctuation are important tools not only for presenting your ideas on paper but for your own thinking on paper as well.

Earlier, when we discussed the generative phases of writing, we stressed the importance of writing in whole sentences on the assumption that the unexpressed idea is often the nonsensical or nonexistent idea (see p. 29). That means writing with subjects, verbs, and predicates in order to ensure that something—anything—actually gets said. It also means inserting some elementary punctuation marks as separators among the different ideas flowing onto the page. Otherwise, it is difficult to tell the difference between an idea articulated and one vaguely alluded to. For example, there is a world of difference at the outset between the one-word sentences "Oh," "Oh!," and "Oh?" Or a vague note like "Vampires, human" might translate into "What are the historical origins of the belief in humanoid vampires?" or "Do Dracula-like vampires exist?" or "I've spoken to Dracula myself!"

Certainly punctuation and grammar become more important the further one gets into the critical, revisionary phases of writing. But like virtually all the other elements of writing, they are minimally present from the beginning. Consider, for instance, the following example of generative writing:

Professor wants essay on standards in learning—don't know
    where to begin
Given or taken
Understood or imposed both
How change with time
In development

Quite all right as a series of cryptic notes just to capture
the flow of ideas, such "word buckshot" quickly loses significance if not soon rewritten (the fate of many class notes,
incidentally). It takes little effort to recast them as follows:

Professor wants ten-page (ds) essay on the role of stan-
    dards in learning. Don't know where to begin. Some
    leading questions:
1. Are standards given or taken; I mean, how do we get
    them?
2. Are standards first imposed and then understood or
    the reverse? Can it go both ways?
3. How do standards change with increasing compe-
    tence?

Writing in whole sentences with punctuation makes all
the difference between these two versions, the latter
amounting almost to an essay outline. Hence, basic grammar and punctuation are anything but mere last-minute trim;
they are part of writing technique from the start.

Let us begin with punctuation and the purposes it serves.

PUNCTUATION

A convenient way of thinking about punctuation is as the
visual equivalent of spoken intonation, as symbolizing the
pauses, stops, and stresses that contribute so much to our
meaning. Punctuation captures much of the rhythm of speech

as well as visually dividing the printed or written page into digestible segments.

The Period

A period is used after all declarative sentences, mild imperatives, and indirect questions, and in some abbreviations.

> **Love is a many-splattered thing.**
> **Love me or leave me. [Or use "!" for greater emphasis.]**
> **She asked if the lawn flamingo was the provincial bird of New Brunswick.**
> **Ph.D., M.D., Mr., Mrs., Jr., Sr., A.M., P.M., A.D., B.C., i.e.**

Omit the periods from most institutional abbreviations (*UCLA, IRS, USMC, WGBH*) and from most technical terms (*H_2O, RFD, stats*).

In outlines: Use a period after the letters or numerals in an outline but not after the heading, unless the heading is on the same line as the following text matter.

> **A. Laughter**
> **1. Its causes and cures**

In ellipses: Three spaced periods are used to indicate an omission at the beginning of or within quoted material. Use four periods when there's an omission at the end of a sentence but the sentence remains grammatically complete; use three periods when only an incomplete fragment remains.

> **Failure too is a kind of death: the furniture sold, the drawers emptied, the removal van waiting like a hearse in the lane to take one to a less expensive destination.**
> **—GRAHAM GREENE**
> **Failure too is a kind of death . . . the removal van waiting like a hearse in the lane. . . .**
> **Failure too is . . .**

In parentheses and quotations: A period belongs within the parentheses of an independent sentence. (That could hardly be more obvious.) A period belongs outside the parentheses enclosed within a larger sentence (and that too could hardly be more obvious). Keep the period inside quoted material.

"The period," she said, "is a strange object."
How strange to speak of the period as an "object."

But omit the period from quoted material within a larger sentence.

N. R. Hanson's stabbing statement "Life is ugly, brutish, and short and should be lived to the hilt" is not an invitation to profligacy.

The Comma

Compared to the period or full stop, the comma is a half stop and separator of items that might be confusing if run together. Rather like the demicadence in music, the placing of commas can sometimes be read off from the sound of the sentence ("Well, I think so"). Clarity and structure are better guides, however, and a few of the more common uses are illustrated below.

Between independent clauses: Commas are used between independent clauses of about equal length and import, especially where a period would break the continuity of thought.

Veni, vidi, vici.
[Instead of] I came. I saw. I conquered.

Between main (independent) clauses joined by connectives like *and, but, for, nor, or, so, yet:* A comma belongs before the connective in all such cases.

The chairman blustered, but the stocks fell anyway.
Ah yes, but have you thought of looking for another position?
The question was shocking, yet it was not unexpected.

But do not separate compound predicates.

The board members got up from their chairs and stalked from the room.

And do not separate compound subjects.

The chairman and the board members got up from their chairs but then sat down again.

After introductory phrases:

As Freud said, much is won if we succeed in transforming hysterical misery into common unhappiness.
Arriving on the train in a state of common unhappiness, she plunged into a state of hysterical misery at the mere sight of him.
To alleviate guilt, become happy.
In fact, hysterical happiness is one of the moods of manic depression.

To separate items in a series: The items can be a series of adjectives, nouns, or whole phrases. With two items joined by a coordinating conjunction, omit the comma.

Dawn slithered like gray slime over the cold, wet, jagged shore.
I found love, happiness, and solvency at IBM.
She arrived early, worked long, and played late.
We had raw tuna and sea urchin, octopus and salmon, prawns and oysters.

Noncoordinate adjectives: Adjectives that cannot be separated by an *and* are noncoordinate and should not be separated by a comma.

She loved maudlin country and western music.
Not: **She loved maudlin, country and western music.**

(The words *country and western music* form one idea modified by *maudlin*.)

To set off nonrestrictive clauses and parenthetical phrases: A nonrestrictive clause is one that could be omitted without changing the meaning of the main clause.

Darwin's *Origin of the Species, it could be argued,* is a theory less of the origin than of the extinction of species.

The union, *in an ill-tempered outburst,* accused management of seeking its extinction.

Restrictive clauses, however, modify and limit the words they follow and should not be set off by commas.

Businesses *that do not adjust to changing market conditions* court their own extinction.

Tycoons *who parade their origins* are indirectly boasting of their success.

The philosopher *John Dewey* heavily influenced business training as well as public education.

Nonrestrictive appositives: Appositives are words or phrases following a noun or pronoun that serve to identify it. Appositives can be restrictive or nonrestrictive. The examples immediately preceding are all restrictive appositives (they could not be eliminated from the sentence without changing the meaning of the main clause). Nonrestrictive appositives, like other parenthetical phrases, are set off by commas.

Octavius Brooks Frothingham, *a Kant scholar,* wrote an excellent early study of transcendentalism in America.

Chairman of the Board Brooks O. Frothingham, *a descendant of O. B. Frothingham,* was in a transcendental mood.

A bronze statue of Ralph Waldo Emerson, *the American transcendentalist,* sits sagely in Emerson Hall at Harvard University.

The mummified body of Jeremy Bentham, *the father of utilitarianism,* sits splay-legged in a glass case at University College, London.

In coordinate phrases: Coordinate phrases modify the same noun and are set off by commas.

The quarterback's forward pass was longer, *though less accurate,* than the center's backward hike.

The center's obsession with forward progress, *though perhaps less evident,* is no less than the quarterback's.

Some other uses of commas—with *of:*

Margaret Chase Smith, of Maine, was the longest-serving congresswoman.

With parentheses:

Margaret Chase Smith, of Maine (a rural state), was the longest-serving congresswoman.

In direct address:

Margaret Chase Smith, you are the longest-serving congresswoman.

In contrasting phrases:

Everything is what it is, not another thing.

In dates:

July 21, 1984   *But:* 21 July 1984

The comma is the most prevalent and versatile piece of punctuation. Accordingly, its uses are best grasped by example and observation of how good writers use it. If in doubt, consult one of the standard references mentioned in Appendix B.

The Semicolon

The semicolon behaves like a supercomma, mostly separating independent clauses and those with internal punctuation (where yet another comma could be confusing). It is also used for listings of longish elements or to take the place of a coordinating conjunction. The semicolon is thus a convenient device for grouping closely related elements for which the period is too strong and the comma too weak.

Between independent clauses without a coordinating conjunction:

Laughter rang through the hall; the effect was chilling.
Come in; this is your host, Raymond.
Welcome to Transylvania; we need new blood.

Or with a coordinating conjunction (especially adverbs of inference and exception like *hence, therefore, thus, nevertheless, then, indeed,* and *so*):

In fact, whenever B. O. Frothingham chaired the meetings, significant decisions were made; hence, his transcendental moods were effective.
One never knows quite what motivates a man like B. O.

Frothingham; indeed, it hardly matters, so long as he gets results.

In a series of clauses:

It all matters, yes; worries, yes; but none of it deters me. He could not recall ever feeling so sure of another person; that he absolutely must not lose her; that every effort had to be made to avert such a loss.

In a listing containing commas:

The members who attended were Professor Klutz, of Yale; Professor Newt, of the Scripps Institute; and Professor Est, of Stanford.

In explanatory phrases:

Chairman of the Board B. O. Frothingham announced that the search for the Holy Grail would be carried out by a special assistant; namely, Mr. Parsifal, of Wagner Enterprises, Ltd.
Or alternately: . . . a special assistant, namely, Mr. Parsifal . . . a special assistant—namely, Mr. Parsifal . . .

The Colon

The purpose of an introduction is to introduce, and the colon does that with remarkable brevity: ":" As an "anticipator" signaling something immediately to follow, it typically precedes a listing, an explanatory clause, or one that amplifies the preceding clause.

Board Chairman B. O. Frothingham began his remarks on the new line of deodorants as follows: "Many years ago, in the Orient, Lamont Cranston learned the secret hypnotic power of the odorous deodorant."

The consensus: B.O. knows.

With listings and illustrations:

The exotic places in the Orient visited by Lamont Cranston: Scranton, Pennsylvania; Wheeling, West Virginia; and Cranston, Rhode Island.

Do not use the colon where the verb precedes the list.

Cranston's itinerary included Scranton, Pennsylvania; Wheeling, West Virginia; and Cranston, Rhode Island.

Use the colon with closely related explanations or amplifications:

No doubt, B.O. had a nose for such things: for the ultimate deodorant and where to find it.

In salutations:

Dear Mr. Cranston: *Or, less formal:* **Dear Lamont,**

Other uses include biblical citations, between chapter and verse (Matthew 3:16), before book subtitles (*Deodorants: Making Sense of Scents*), in book references (New York: Olfactory Press, 1984), in periodical citations, between the volume and page numbers (*Journal of Smell,* 2:147–151), with plays, between act and scene (*The Nose Knows,* II:2), with time (8:50 P.M.).

The Dash

The primary use of the dash is to create a pregnant pause to show an interruption in thought, to amplify an idea, or to emphasize a parenthetical element.

To emphasize appositives:

The meerschaum—the king of pipes—is a work of art, not just another smoke.

In summary clauses:

She begged, borrowed, and stole—everything she had vowed not to do.
Ted, Alice, Fred, and Jane—all retired early.

To signal breaks in thought:

I asked her—oh, God, did I?—whither progress in the philosophy of John Dewey.
It is well known—or at least widely assumed—that experience is the best preacher.

To indicate authorship of brief quotes:

To be is to be conceived.—BISHOP BERKELEY
To be is to be the value of a bound variable.
—W.V.O. QUINE

The Question Mark
The question mark comes after a direct question or a question within a larger statement.

Where's the oasis?
The question Where's the oasis? was on all our salivating tongues.

But not after an indirect question or polite request.

They all wanted to know where the oasis was.
Will you please be patient.

A question mark is also used to indicate editorial uncertainty or to express irony.

The Greek logician Absurdides (ca. 450 B.C.?) spoke only in contradictions.
Absurdides is an inspiration(?) to many contemporary politicians.

The Exclamation Mark

The exclamation mark registers surprise, disbelief, or other strong emotions. Like a loud voice, it is quickly annoying if overused.

I say! You are something to behold!
You must be joking!
Ouch!

The exclamation mark is also used after commands and to indicate irony.

Arm the presents! I mean, present arms!
Now there's a sergeant with presence(!) of mind.

Brackets, Parentheses, and Slashes

Brackets are mainly used to insert editorial remarks within quoted material, to indicate corrections, and to issue directions.

Unlike Margaret Budd—whose married name I could not remember—Bijou Ardglass [mistress of Prince Theodoric] appeared distinctly older: more than a little ravaged by the demands of her existence.—ANTHONY POWELL
Immanuel Cant [Kant] wrote the *Critique of Pure Reason.*

Or: Immanuel Cant [sic] . . .
[Turn to next page]   [To be continued]
NICK *[suddenly surprised]: Who, me?*

Parentheses are parenthetical: for enclosing clarifying, explanatory, or nonessential material.

Within a fortnight (March 31) the prime minister of Great Britain had resigned.
The reasons proffered in his resignation speech (pp. 3–4) were unconvincing.
The politics of the situation (or so one surmises) prevented candor.

Parentheses also enclose numbers or letters in a series within a continuous text.

The prime minister offered as reasons (a) that his government had lost the confidence of the people; (b) that his party no longer supported him; and (c) that he disliked the strawberry ice cream served at No. 10 Downing Street.

A parenthetical sentence within a sentence omits the capital letter at the beginning and the period at the end. An independent parenthetical sentence is fully punctuated.

She was churlish under questioning (in a funk, she turned away from the microphones) and not a little arrogant.
A minute passed. (It seemed an eternity.)

The slash indicates alternatives and sequences.

The voting options (pro/con/abstain) leave no room for qualified support.
The forecast: The day/night cycle will continue with in-

creasing darkness toward nightfall followed by brightness toward dawn.

The slash also indicates footing in poetry contained in a running text.

The lines, as I recall them, ran, "The sun is setting in the wine/Caught in its crystal glass/Both yours and mine. . . ."

Quotation Marks

Quotation marks are preservers. They mention other discourse while preserving the exact words of the original. They enclose all direct quotations, some references to titles (of paintings, chapters, songs, articles, and so on), some technical words, and unusual slang expressions.

"Who knows what evil lurks in the hearts of men?" he asked.

But do not use quotation marks with indirect quotation.

He replied that the Shadow knows.

With names and titles:

"Guernica" was Picasso's protest against the savagery of war.
Chapter V, "The Uncivil Painter," explores Picasso's attitudes toward established authority.

With technical and slang expressions:

The words "work," "force," and "mass" lose their ordinary meanings in physics.
He asked her what kind of "slug" she thought he was.

Quotations within quotations: Single quotes enclose a quotation with a larger quotation.

"I recall reading it," he said, "on a gallery poster entitled 'Reflections.' "

Question marks and exclamation marks belong inside quotation marks only when they are part of the original statement; otherwise outside.

"Where are they?" he asked.
Can we afford to "consult all interested parties"?

Again, in American English commas and periods belong inside the quotation marks (in British English, outside). Semicolons and colons belong outside. Otherwise they are dropped from within the quotation.

The Apostrophe
The apostrophe indicates possession and certain contractions and plurals.

I could see the ship's sail slapping in the wind.
I could see all the ships' sails slapping in the wind.
Where's (where is) the beef? It's (it is) here.
But: Its (the meat's) quality is questionable.
The woman asking the question appears to be in her 80's.
That would put her in the class of '19 or '20.

GRAMMAR
Grammar concerns how words function in sentences. That function has two parts: how words contribute to the structure of a sentence, and how they refer to things (including other words). Seen in this light, grammatical conventions,

though often arbitrary (like driving on the left or the right side of the road), assist in the precise expression of ideas. They give us both the hope and the means of *saying* what we mean in orderly and exact ways, mostly by eliminating potential sources of confusion. As with punctuation, we present here the minimum in self-defense against the more common errors of grammar and sentence structure.

From Words to Sentences

You cannot grasp how or what words mean until you understand how they are used in sentences. Like actors in a play, words can and do play many different roles called parts of speech. Dictionaries, then, are like "program notes" on the acting careers of particular words. Words are classified into eight parts of speech according to how they are used in sentences: nouns, pronouns, verbs, adverbs, adjectives, prepositions, conjunctions, and interjections. And as said, many words play different parts depending on how they are used. For example:

> The concept of *value* is moot. [noun]
> I *value* her opinion. [verb]
> That is a *value* problem. [adjective]

Nouns name things—anything: persons (*George*), events (*World War II*), objects (*roses, toes*), places (*London*), feelings (*melancholy, ecstasy*), abstractions (*love, democracy, existentialism*), and so forth.

Pronouns promote economy of expression by standing in for nouns and their attendant words.

> *The long-faced, woolly-headed chairman of the board* took *his* place at the head of the table.
> *The hurricane* struck. *It* was ferocious.
> *Fred and Alice* were the only board members to retain *their* composure.

Verbs function as predicates or parts of predicates of sentences. They say something about the subject of the sentence. The verb is therefore the key—the turning point—of every sentence, linking its two basic elements.

Alice *tripped.*
Alice *tripped* through the looking glass.
Alice *was tripped up* by the March Hare.

The last example illustrates the verb phrase consisting of an auxiliary verb plus a main verb (e.g., *will try, had gone, has moved, were thinking, have taken*). Verbs express actions taken or undergone, happenings, identity, and states of being. They *are* the "movers" of every sentence.

Adverbs modify verbs. They also modify adjectives and other adverbs. Mostly, they indicate how, when, where, or to what extent something is done or obtains. For example:

Alice tripped *gaily* through the looking glass. [modifies the verb *tripped*]
Alice tripped *exceedingly* gaily through the looking glass. [modifies the adverb *gaily*]
Alice tripped through the *most* unusual looking glass. [modifies the adjective *unusual*]

The ending *-ly* usually(!) converts an adjective to an adverb: *practical/practically, beautiful/beautifully, honest/honestly.*

Finally, an adverb may modify an entire sentence or clause. An adverb can *really* achieve that much.

Adjectives describe, limit, or qualify nouns and pronouns, thus sharing with adverbs the task of modifying other words. The most common adjectives are the definite (*the*) and indefinite (*a, an*) articles: *the* peach, *an* apple, *a* pear. Adjectives are also descriptive (*bold* idea, *quick brown* fox, *hopeless* proposition), interrogative (*what* idea? *which* fox? *whose* proposition?), numerical (*one* idea, *two* foxes), and demonstrative (*this* idea, *that* fox, *these* propositions, *those* hopeless propositions). Usually coming before the nouns or pronouns they modify, adjectives are the most common qualifiers we have.

Prepositions always take an object; that is, they relate nouns and pronouns to other words. A list of common prepositions includes *of, at, with, above, across, during, under, in, on, into, off, near, inside, outside, over, behind, below, like, through, within, without, until, toward, beyond, since, up, down.* Compound prepositions include *instead of, out of, contrary to, in spite of, because of, for the sake of.* A prepositional phrase consists of a preposition and its object. For example:

For Abelard's sake, Heloise betook herself to a nunnery.
Theirs was a love affair *of grandiose proportions.*

Conjunctions connect words, phrases, or clauses (a clause differing from a phrase in having both a subject and a predicate). Conjunctions fall into three classes. Coordinating conjunctions (*and, or, but, yet, neither-nor*) connect items of equal importance in a sentence.

Abelard *and* Heloise were in love.
Abelard *and* Heloise were in love, *but* Abelard was a priestly philosopher.
***Neither* love *nor* money could save them.**

Subordinating conjunctions connect subordinate clauses with main clauses using words like *when, where, while, since, because, if,* and the like:

***If* Abelard and Heloise had been more discrete, they might have gotten away with it.**

Because of their passionate correspondence, they were found out.

Conjunctive adverbs connect independent clauses that could be separate sentences. The most common conjunctive adverbs are *therefore, however, nonetheless, consequently, besides, also, otherwise,* and *moreover.*

The church authorities were in high dudgeon; *nonetheless,* Heloise and Abelard persisted.
They were consumed by their passion. *Consequently,* they paid the price.
Their letters attest to the honesty of their moral conflict; *otherwise,* they should have been more "discrete."

Interjections are exclamatory words (often followed by an exclamation mark), and usually stand alone.

"*Oh!* I cannot take this lying down," said Abelard.
"*Well!* You may have to," said Heloise.

Sentences are conveniently classified into four kinds: The simple sentence contains one independent clause.

The world turns.

The compound sentence contains at least two independent clauses.

The world turns, life goes on, and who's the wiser?

The complex sentence contains one or more dependent clauses and one independent clause.

As the world turns, as life goes on, some get wiser.

The compound-complex sentence consists of a compound sentence and one or more dependent clauses.

As the world turns, as life goes on, some get wiser and some don't.

Note that in some of the examples above, the subordinating conjunction *as* converts the independent clauses *the world turns* and *life goes on* into dependent clauses incapable of standing alone. That brings us to the first glaring error of grammar to avoid.

The Sentence Fragment
The sentence fragment is an incomplete sentence punctuated as a complete sentence. Some are obvious, some not. As the immediately preceding examples show, the mere presence of a subject and predicate is necessary but insufficient to determine whether something is a sentence.

Wrong: **As the world turns.**
Right: **The world turns.**
Right: **As the world turns, life goes on.**

What the last example shows is that to become a sentence, a fragment must be joined to a main clause. Some other examples of fragments rewritten as sentences:

Fragments: **However much he talked about the subject. There was very little he was prepared to do.**
Sentence: **However much he talked about the subject, there was very little he was prepared to do.**
Fragments: **In one sense novelists are unsatisfactory critics of other novelists' work. Because they always feel that they themselves would have written any given novel another way.**

Sentence: In one sense novelists are unsatisfactory critics of other novelists' work, because they always feel that they themselves would have written any given novel another way. —ANTHONY POWELL

Fragments: He did not want those following him to give up the hunt. Merely to be slowed down. Separated if possible. If he could trap one, that would be ideal.

Sentence: He did not want those following him to give up the hunt, merely to be slowed down, separated if possible; if he could trap one, that would be ideal. —ROBERT LUDLUM

There are times, however, when the deliberate use of fragments can be as effective as the unwitting occurrence of them embarrassing. There is no hard-and-fast rule. For example, to eliminate the fragments from the following would be to lose the urgency of the thought.

Have I been preparing myself for a new journey? Secretly? Beneath the layers of defensive resistance? Possibly.

The Comma Splice

The comma splice results from two independent sentences being joined by a comma rather than separated by a period or joined by a coordinating conjunction or semicolon. The effect is to muddle the differences as well as the relations between the two sentences. Some examples of comma splices and their corrections:

Comma splice: The years of underground burrowings, of secret or disguised preparations were now over, Hitler at length felt himself strong enough to make his first open challenge.

Correction: The years of underground burrowings, of secret or disguised preparations were now over, and Hitler at length felt himself strong enough to make his first open challenge. —WINSTON CHURCHILL

Alternative: The years of underground burrowings, of secret or disguised preparations were now over. Hitler at length felt himself strong enough to make his first open challenge.

Comma splice: It was the first Greek he had heard spoken for some time, it filled him with a kind of nostalgic pain.

Correction: It was the first Greek he had heard spoken for some time; it filled him with a kind of nostalgic pain. —LAWRENCE DURRELL

Comma splices often result from the insertion of a conjunctive adverb like *hence, therefore, accordingly, moreover,* or *afterward* between two independent clauses.

Comma splice: The order that our mind imagines is like a net, or like a ladder, built to attain something, afterward you must throw the ladder away, because you discover that, even if it was useful, it was meaningless.

Correction: The order that our mind imagines is like a net, or like a ladder, built to attain something. But afterward you must throw the ladder away, because you discover that, even if it was useful, it was meaningless. —UMBERTO ECO

Still, there are exceptions for short, evenly balanced phrases:

I think, therefore I am.
She loves me, she loves me not.
Act in haste, repent at leisure.

Active Versus Passive Sentences

Clear sentence structure results from writing in active rather than passive sentences wherever possible. That means using a verb of doing to express action rather than a noun plus a verb of being, e.g., "We *recommend* that . . ." versus "The *recommendation is* that . . ." To avoid passive constructions: (1) Put the subject matter or acting agent in the subject place of the sentence; (2) place the verb expressing action taken or undergone as close to the subject as possible; and (3) avoid those constructions that make the subject or agent the passive object of action rather than taking action. As the "first rule" of clear writing, the placing of active verbs in close proximity to their subjects goes far toward eliminating the more common sources of error and obscurity. Consider the following sentence:

It was determined that information was insufficient for the committee to recommend specific action on the question of housing needs for the elderly in the designated area.

The sentence commits no grammatical errors; it is simply unwieldy and obscure. For instance, who determined that the information was insufficient? Is the action to be taken on the question of needs or on the needs themselves? Is there any difference between taking specific action and just taking action? Does *housing needs* refer to improvements in existing housing or new housing? The sentence gains clarity and directness when cast in the active voice.

The committee lacked sufficient information to recommend any action on housing for the elderly in that area.

A further gain comes from eliminating the redundant phrase *any action on* and adding more details.

The committee lacked enough information to recommend housing improvements for the elderly in the Bathurst area.

Passivity often results from the use of abstract nouns rather than verbs to express action (e.g., *determination/determines, action/acts*) and from various uses of the verb *to be* to assert the existence of the action rather than expressing it directly. Some examples:

Passive: A determination of the feasibility of new market-development areas has been made by Mr. Parsifal of Wagner Enterprises, Ltd.
Active: Mr. Parsifal of Wagner Enterprises, Ltd., determined the feasibility of entering new markets.
Or: Mr. Parsifal of Wagner Enterprises, Ltd., researched possible new markets.

Passive: It was found that a need exists for Holy Grail authentication procedures.
Active: We need to authenticate the Holy Grail.

Passive: A review was conducted by Mr. Parsifal of potential new markets for holy relics, and we had a discussion of the matter.
Active: Mr. Parsifal reviewed the holy-relics market, and we discussed the matter.

The impulse to "formalize" one's prose, to be portentous, or to appear "objective" accounts for a lot of the pompous language emanating from public figures, bureaucracies, and institutions. Such persiflage is felt by the authors to indicate the existence of a need for an effective active-verb use promotion policy(!).

Agreement of Subjects and Verbs

Agreement refers to the consistency of number—whether singular or plural—between subjects and verbs and between pronouns and their antecedents. Disagreement of both kinds is one of the most common errors of English usage. Pronominal agreement will be discussed under the general heading of pronominal reference in the next section.

The rule of agreement is simple enough: Singular subjects take singular verbs; plural subjects take plural verbs. It's the application that is tricky, especially where intervening nouns and pronouns separate the subject from the verb in longish sentences.

Moby Dick by Herman Melville *is* no mere big-fish story. The whalers aboard the *Pequod* *are* no mere deckhands.

Compound subjects linked by *and* are usually plural.

Moby Dick and the crew of the *Pequod* *were* joined in mortal combat.

But compound subjects referring to a single entity are singular.

The captain of the *Pequod* and nemesis of Moby Dick *was* Ahab.

Either . . . or and *neither . . . nor* in a compound subject usually take a singular verb unless the subject nearest the verb is plural.

Either Ahab or the White Whale *was* to prevail. Neither whaling nor whales *exhaust* the deeper meaning of the tale.

Neither whales nor whaling *exhausts* the deeper meaning of the tale.

Used as subjects, *either, neither, each, one, anyone, everyone* take singular verbs. *All, any, some, none* may take singular or plural verbs depending on the context.

Each *has* a role to play in the drama.
By the end of the tale, all [everything] *is* lost.
None *survive* [compare: no one *survives*]; all *are* lost, save Ishmael who alone *survives* "to tell thee."
However, some of the story *is* told by the Universal Observer (Melville).

A collective noun or quantity takes a singular verb when treated as a unit, a plural verb when treated as a collection of individuals.

On the eve of the chase, the crew *pledges* its loyalty to Ahab.
A small cabal, led by the first mate, [it] *is* skeptical.
The cabal [they] *think* Ahab may be mad.
The number of recalcitrants *is* very small.
A number of the crew *are* fanatically zealous.

Some nouns are plural in form but singular in meaning and take a singular verb: *economics, news, athletics,* and so forth.

Here *is* the latest news: Aquatics *is* not Ahab's sport.

Pronominal Reference
Pronominal reference concerns both the agreement and the accuracy of reference by pronouns to their antecedents.

Disagreement and vague reference of pronouns are constant threats to clarity.

The rule of agreement is the same for pronouns and their antecedents as for subjects and verbs: singular antecedent, singular pronoun; plural antecedent, plural pronoun.

> **Clutching the *bathrobe* across her breasts, she shifts and sits upright; then tucks *it* under her armpits.**
>
> —JOHN FOWLES
>
> **I suppose that's why *people* become scientists—*they* can't stand the chaos of the ordinary world   —COLIN WILSON**

Relative pronouns like *who, whom, which, what, that* used as subjects take singular or plural verbs according to the number of their antecedents.

> **It is *they who shift and sit* upright.**
> ***Dissatisfaction* with the chaos of the ordinary world is *what makes* scientists.**

Either, neither, each, one, anyone, everybody usually take singular pronouns.

> **Neither vice-president of the firm received *his/her* invitation to the gala.**
> **Anyone admitted was required to show *his or her* invitation.**
> **Each social gaff had *its* repercussions.**

Everybody, everyone, a person sometimes take plural pronouns when the reference is general.

> **Everybody gets overlooked sometime, but *they* don't take it all so seriously.**
> ***But not*: One has to have enough confidence in *them-***

selves to take it lightly. [Inconsistent reference; use *one-self.*]

Singular or plural pronouns are used with collective nouns depending upon whether the verb is singular or plural. Avoid inconsistencies like the following:

The social committee *is* writing *their* apologies. [Use *its apologies* to be consistent with the singular verb.]
The offended group *are* writing *its* own versions of the snafu. [Use *their own versions.*]
Labor *is* also aggrieved; *they too are* inconsolable. [Use *it too is.*]

Singular antecedents joined by *and* take a plural pro-noun. Antecedents joined by *either . . . or* or *neither . . . nor* take a singular pronoun unless the nearest antecedent is plural.

Fred and Alice voiced *their* hopes for amelioration.
Neither cakes nor ale had [has] *its* desired effect.
Neither ale nor cakes had [have] *their* desired effect.

Ambiguous reference occurs when it is unclear to which antecedent a pronoun refers. In this, as in other cases of confused reference, the best remedy is to repeat the ante-cedent or use a synonym.

Ambiguous: The social committee was caught by Fred and Alice with their pants down. [Embarrassing for Fred and Alice!]
Unambiguous: Fred and Alice caught the social commit-tee with its pants down.
Or: The social committee was caught with its pants down by Fred and Alice.

Vague reference occurs when the pronoun is placed so far from its antecedent that the reader is left unsure what it refers to (like the last *it* in this sentence, referring to *pronoun*). Rewrite the sentence repeating the antecedent:

Clearer: Vague reference occurs when the pronoun is placed so far from its antecedent that the reader is left unsure what that pronoun refers to.
Or: . . . unsure about the pronoun's reference.

Another remedy is to move the pronoun closer to its antecedent.

Vague: Among her generation of dancers, Martha Graham was renowned for her teaching as well as for her dancing, *who* was a founder of modern dance.
Clearer: Among her generation of dancers, Martha Graham, *who* was a founder of modern dance, was equally renowned for her teaching and for her dancing.

Vague reference also results from the unclear use of a pronoun to refer to a general idea or unexpressed implication.

Vague: Teaching is a difficult, often unrewarding profession requiring patience and skill, not to mention high ideals. *That* applies to other jobs too. [*That* has no clear antecedent.]
Clearer: Teaching is a difficult, often unrewarding profession requiring patience and skill, not to mention high ideals. Similar difficulties and demands occur in other professions.

Vague: Becoming an educated person oneself is the first task of an aspiring teacher; otherwise, it is liable to drift into mere routine. [*It* presumably refers to the implied notion of *teaching.*]

Clearer: Becoming an educated person oneself is the first task of an aspiring teacher; otherwise, teaching [or, *the teacher*] is liable to drift into mere routine.

Certain awkwardnesses result from overworking *it*, first as an expletive, then as a pronoun, within the same sentence.

Awkward: If it is a wise policy to focus on the education of teachers, it is no good unless it is backed by greater financial incentives.

Less choppy: The wise policy of focusing on teacher education will fail unless backed by greater financial incentives.

Or: Though the policy of emphasizing the education of teachers is wise, it will fail if not backed by greater financial incentives.

COMMON ERRORS OF WORD USAGE

Following is an alphabetical selection of the more common errors of word usage. A good dictionary is your best guide to proper usage, but only if you are alert to the possibility of a mistake. The more common errors of word usage tend to slip by us like ingrained bad habits; others notice them when we fail to.

The selection below represents only the most recurrent errors encountered. The format and many of the errors are the same as in the glossary of usage (Section 19i) in the *Harbrace College Handbook.* Another good, short reference on usage is Chapter 9, "Style and Usage," in Joseph M. Williams's *Style: Ten Lessons in Clarity and Grace* (see Appendix B).

a, an   Two forms of the indefinite article, *a* coming before a consonant sound, *an* before a vowel sound.

an osprey, *an* opening, *an* abacus, *an* honor, *a* hotel, *a*
wish, *a* one-horse show

accept, except   The verb *accept* means "to receive" or
"to consent"; the preposition *except* means "to leave out
or exclude."

We *accept* your criticism.
We *accept* your criticism *except* for the implication of
blame.

affect, effect   The verb *affect* means "to influence or
change." The noun *affect* means "emotion." The noun *effect*
means "something brought about by a cause," a result.

Polls seem to *affect* voters' choices.
High *affect* permeated the campaign.
The *effect* was confusing.

all right, alright   *All right* means "satisfactory," "correct."
Alright is nonstandard spelling.

Alright is not quite all right.

already, all ready   The adverb *already* means "by a specified time." *All ready* means "entirely prepared."

The boat had *already* left.
So there I was, *all ready* and no place to go.

altogether, all together   The adverb *altogether* means
"entirely." *All together* means "in a group."

She was *altogether* pleased.
But we were not *all together.*

among, between   The preposition *among* means "in the midst of" or "in the company of." It implies more than two, whereas *between* implies only two.

She was a princess *among* women.
Between you and me, one wonders.

anyone, any one   *Anyone* means "any person." *Any one* means "any one of a specified group."

Not *anyone* can run a sub-four-minute mile.
Any one of the top ten milers in the world can run a sub-four-minute mile.

as, like   Generally *as, as if, as though* function as conjunctions (*as* sweet *as* honey, acting *as if* he were crazy, *as though* it were a fact). *Like* is usually a preposition expressing similarity, manner, or disposition (like me, *like* a fox, feel *like* dancing, looks *like* rain). Avoid using *like* as a conjunction in formal speech and writing.

Not: Winstons taste good *like* a cigarette should.
But: Winstons taste good *as* a cigarette should.

Not: She looked *like* she was angry.
But: She looked *as if* she were angry.

Avoid substituting *as* for *whether, because, since, while,* or other conjunctions.

Not: I am not sure *as* it is true.
But: I am not sure *whether* it is true.

Not: As I was unsure, I did nothing.
But: Because I was unsure, I did nothing.

Not: As the boat was late, we had a drink.
But: Since the boat was late, we had a drink.

can't hardly   Nonstandard for *can hardly.* In general, avoid this and other double negatives listed below.

different from, to, than   *Different from* means "is unlike" or "stands apart from." Avoid substituting the nonstandard phrases *different to* and *different than.*

Not: Marriage is *different than (to)* what I expected.
But: Marriage is *different from* what I expected.

don't, doesn't   *Don't* is the contraction of *do not; doesn't* of *does not.* Don't substitute *don't* for *doesn't* or *does not.* And avoid *don't hardly.*

Wrong: It just *don't* matter.
Wrong: It *don't hardly* matter.
Right: It just *doesn't* matter.

few, fewer; less, lesser   In contrasts involving number or specific quantities, *few* and *fewer* are the preferred terms (*few* participants, *fewer* opportunities). For qualitative contrasts, use *less* and *lesser* (*less* courage, *less* preferred, the *lesser* choice).

good, well   *Good* is usually an adjective, *well* an adverb. Avoid using *good* as an adverb in formal discourse.

He hit him really *good.* [meaning *hard* or *well*]
She interviewed *good.* [meaning *well*]

I don't feel so *good.* [use *well*]
The fire feels so *good.* [adjective modifying *fire*]

hardly, scarcely Avoid the double negatives *can't hardly*
and *don't scarcely;* in English, one negative is enough.

Not: I *can't hardly* tell.
But: I *can hardly* tell.

hopefully *Hopefully* is an adverb (as in *spoke hopefully
of the matter*), but avoid its all too common use as a conjunctive adverb (as in *hopefully, we shall*). The advice is controversial given the popularity of the latter usage. But be
assured that a careful editor will pick you up on it. So:

Not: Hopefully, I will attend.
But: I *hope* to be able to attend.

imply, infer To *imply* means "to suggest" or "to hint."
To *infer* means "to deduce" or to draw a conclusion." Hence:

He *implied* that something was amiss.
She *inferred* that it concerned herself.

irregardless An especially egregious error (likely originating in a confusion with *irrespective,* a perfectly respectable word); so avoid it. Use *regardless.*

its, it's A bit confusing, but *its* is the possessive ("The
heart has *its* reasons"); *it's* is the contraction of *it is* ("*It's*
Superman!").

lay, lie A vexatious duo; the trick is to remember that
lay is a transitive verb (one that always takes an object),
whereas *lie* is intransitive.

He wanted *to lay* his hand on her arm. [infinitive]
He *is laying* his hand on her arm. [present participle]
He *laid* his hand on her arm. [past tense]
He *has laid* his hand on her arm. [past participle]

I want *to lie* down. [infinitive]
I *am lying* down. [present participle]
I *lay* down. [past tense]
I *have lain* down. [past participle]

me, I   *Me,* along with *us, him, her, them,* and *whom,* is
an objective pronoun, usually the object of a preposition (*to
me, with us, from her, to whom*). *I,* along with *we, he, she,
they,* and *who,* is a subjective pronoun, usually the subject
of a verb (*I ran, she stayed, who can*). Problems arise with
compound constructions like the following. When in doubt,
look for the verb or preposition that goes with the pronoun
in question.

He and *I* fled to Cambridge. [not *him* and *me*]
They came with *him* and *me.* [objects of preposition;
not *him* and *I*]
For *him* and *me,* it was a relief. [objects of preposition;
not *he* and *I*]
No one objected to the trip but *he* and *she.* [subject
complements: *he and she objected;* not *him* and *her*]
This is *she who* objected. [subjects; not *her who*]
She wanted to speak to *him* and *me.* [objects; not *him
and I* or *he and I*]
With *whom* did she actually speak? [object; not *with who*]
She spoke to *us* Cambridge people. [object; not *we Cambridge people*]
She wondered whether it was *they* or *we* who had fled
to Cambridge. [subjects; *they or we who had fled;* not *them
or us*]

She is someone *whom* we distrust. [object of verb: *distrust whom;* not *who we distrust*]
She is someone *who* we know is untrustworthy. [subject of verb: *who is untrustworthy*]
He loathes her far more than *I* (loathe her). [subject; not *more than me*]

principal, principle *Principal* means "foremost in importance" or "leading personage"; *principle* means "basic truth or assumption." Hence:

The *principal* was utterly without *principles.*
That was the *principal* reason for his dismissal.

real, really Avoid substituting the adjective *real* for the adverb *really* or using *real* to mean "very" or "extremely."

Wrong: He hit him *real good.*
Right: He hit him *really well.* [or *really hard*]
Wrong: His opponent was *real* hurt.
Right: His opponent was *badly* hurt. [*very, extremely*]

rise, raise *Rise* is intransitive; *raise* is transitive. Hence:

I *rise* (*rose, have risen*) earlier in the country than in the city.
That *raises* (*raised, has raised*) a scheduling problem.

set, sit *Set,* like *lay,* takes an object; *sit,* like *lie,* does not. That is, *set* is transitive, *sit* is not. Hence:

He *sits* (*is sitting, sat, has sat*) on his hands.
She *sets* (*is sitting, set, has set*) the table.
In so doing they both *set* traps for each other.

than, then   *Than* is a conjunction; *then* an adverb relating to time or consequence.

It gets your clothes whiter *than* white!
How white, *then,* is that?
Whiter *than* before?
Right, whiter *than then*!

they're, their, there   A troublesome trio frequently confused. *They're* is the contraction of *they are*. *Their* is a possessive pronoun. *There* is an adverb (*in there*) or expletive (*there is, there are*).

They're up to *their* old tricks over *there.*

try and   *Try to* avoid it in writing.

which, that   Among relative pronouns, *which* introduces nonrestrictive, "commenting" clauses, while *that* introduces restrictive, "defining" clauses. Recall that nonrestrictive clauses can be omitted from a sentence without changing its basic meaning, whereas restrictive clauses limit the subject of the sentence in ways that do affect the basic meaning (see pp. 103–104 above).

Deer Island, *which* is in the Bay of Fundy, is one of several Westerly Isles. [commenting clause]
The island *that* Roosevelt called his "beloved island" is nearby Campobello Island. [defining clause]
Roosevelt's summer home, *which* is now an international park, is on Campobello. [commenting clause]
The house, *which* faces west, belies the play *that* is called *Sunrise at Campobello.* [commenting and defining clauses respectively]

Often it is better simply to omit gratuitous pronouns. For example:

The house, which faces west, belies the play called *Sunrise at Campobello*.

who, whom   See **me, I** above.

DOING THE CHORES ON THE WORD FARM

After this welter of dos and don'ts of punctuation and grammar, you may be longing for some simple, strategic guidance. Forty years ago, in his "Politics and the English Language," George Orwell offered just such guidance in no uncertain terms (1946, p. 139). We cannot improve upon his advice.

   i. Never use a metaphor, simile or other figure of speech which you are used to seeing in print.

  ii. Never use a long word where a short one will do.

 iii. If it is possible to cut a word out, always cut it out.

 iv. Never use the passive where you can use the active [voice].

  v. Never use a foreign phrase, a scientific word or a jargon word if you can think of an everyday English equivalent.

 vi. Break any of these rules sooner than say anything outright barbarous.

APPENDIX A

Deductive and Inductive Reasoning

THE NATURE OF DEDUCTION AND INDUCTION

Deduction and induction are forms of inference, ways of connecting up statements to make arguments; that is, ways of relating statements as *reasons* or *evidence* to the conclusions drawn. Without these connections between ideas our minds would be reduced to a random collection of isolated beliefs and perceptions, none of which related, except by chance association, to any other. This is another way of saying that deductive and inductive reasoning are part of the fabric of common sense and everyday experience.*

Deductive and inductive *logic* are the formalized rules and principles of inference abstracted from sound reasoning itself, including its more rarefied forms in science and mathematics. Thus the rules of logic are both descriptive and prescriptive of how rational inferences *should* be made. They articulate the principles we implicitly observe in sound rea-

*For an excellent, accessible survey of these and other matters pertaining to reasoning in general, see Raymond S. Nickerson's *Notes About Reasoning* (Cambridge, Mass.: Bolt, Beranek, and Neman Report No. 5191, November 1982). Available from BB&N, 10 Moulton Street, Cambridge, MA 02238. Many of Nickerson's observations on reasoning are woven into the present brief account.

soning of any kind. To that extent, they resemble rules of grammar abstracted from what is presumed to be the proper use of language. And as with rules of grammar, to be able to use them in practice you don't need to know them all or have full mastery of them *as abstractions.*

Deductive inference is from a given, an assumption. This means that if the premises are true and the inference is valid, then the conclusion must also be true. That leaves open whether the premises are true, for a valid deduction can be drawn from falsehoods. (Common sense is often misled in exactly that way.)

For example, if I infer "Luiz dances the samba" from the premises "All Brazilians dance the samba" and "Luiz is a Brazilian," the inference is *valid.* The conclusion could not be otherwise given these premises, whether or not they are true. There you have the litmus test of valid deductive inference: The conclusion is *necessarily* true if (and that's always a big if) the premises from which it is drawn are also true.

On the other hand, if I infer "Luiz is a Brazilian" from the facts (assuming they are such) that "Luiz dances the samba" and "All Brazilians dance the samba," the inference is *invalid* even if, in fact, Luiz turns out to be a Brazilian. That illustrates the difference between validity and truth; namely, that a conclusion can be true though invalidly inferred and false where validly inferred. All we can be sure of with a deductive inference is that *if* the premises are true, *and* the argument is valid, *then* the conclusion must also be true.

The fallacy involved in inferring "Luiz is a Brazilian" from the above premises is called the fallacy of affirming the consequent: *If A then B, B, therefore A.* Can you spot why it is a fallacy? Why the conclusion does not follow necessarily? Plug in other statements for the variables *A* and *B* until the idea sinks in.

The two most basic "laws" of deductive reasoning are the law of noncontradiction (*Not both A and not A*) and the law of excluded middle (*Either A or not A but not both*). Two other logical principles constantly used by us all have been called since ancient times *modus ponens* and *modus tollens.* In scheme they look like this respectively: *If A then B, A, therefore B;* and *If A then B, not B, therefore not A.* Make up examples from these by substituting statements for the variables and you will discover a wealth of "classical" knowledge you may have been unaware of possessing. For instance, "If she loves me, then I'm a monkey's uncle." Which of the above principles does that statement (with its implicit conclusion) fit?

Induction is reasoning evidentially, from facts, by inferences that are plausible or probable, not necessary. An interesting thing about induction is that by deductive standards, it appears invalid. It seems always to be committing the fallacy of affirming the consequent or drawing a universal ("all") conclusion from a finite ("some") premise. For instance, the inference that "all emeralds are green" is based upon observations that *cannot* have included *all* emeralds past, present, and future.

Or consider this more complicated example. Using Kepler's laws of planetary motion, if one were to infer that the array of the planets today at time t must be thus and so, because three weeks ago they were such and so at t *minus 3,* that is a valid deductive inference. The conclusion follows necessarily from the statements of the laws themselves (whether or not the planets actually are thus and so today). If, on the other hand, one were to *observe* that indeed the array of the planets at time t today *is* thus and so and infer from that the *truth* of Kepler's laws, that would be affirming the consequent, would it not? Even if one made hundreds of similar "confirming" observations at different times, all of them precisely as predicted, the argument still has the (deductively) invalid form of *If A then B, B, therefore A.* Similarly, were one to conclude that seeds of the giant sequoia tree mature in the second season, because all seeds observed *thus far* have matured in the second season, is that not an unwarranted inference from "some" to "all" (unobserved past and future seeds)?

Obviously something has gone wrong here if basic scientific method turns out to be "invalid," so the answer cannot be a simple yes or no. The point is that deductive and inductive inference are different. The validity of the one cannot be measured by the standards of the other. Two plus two does not equal four on *evidence*. Nor are Kepler's laws true of planetary motion simply because they hang together in a tightly deductive system.*

Medieval science assumed just that: that a system of deductively valid statements must also be *empirically true,* true in fact. Taking the deductive model of geometry as the measure of all reliable knowledge of the natural world, early thinkers made of science a purely logical exercise cut off from facts, observation, and experiment.

Deductive consistency and coherence became the touchstones of real knowledge, not the "probabalism" of fallible facts and observations. By that standard, Pope Urban VIII was more than justified in not accepting Galileo's invitation to observe the true face of the heavens through the latter's telescope! Faith and pure reason were the pope's measures of truth, not the clutter of experience. "Don't trouble me with facts" is the motto of a purely deductive science.

But of course science, and common sense too, are not purely deductive. We are much troubled, informed, and led by what we experience and observe. Induction begins there—with the ability to *generalize,* with the ability to infer gen-

---

*For further details on the differences between deduction and induction, including a splendid exposé of commonplace misunderstandings of both, see Brian Skyrms's *Choice and Chance: An Introduction to Inductive Logic* (Belmont, Calif.: Dickenson Publishing Company, 1966); especially Chapter 1, "Probability and Induction." Skyrms's text is short, thorough, and crystal clear—useful to both beginners and advanced students of induction.

eral principles and to make predictions based upon a *selection* of facts. We routinely induce hypotheses, explanations, covariances, and probabilities from what we observe—from predicting the weather to predicting the paths of subatomic particles in a Wilson cloud chamber.

There are as many patterns of inductive as of deductive inference. For instance, observing that the members of a certain class *A* have a property *B,* and observing no exceptions over many observations, we may infer that *all A's are B's;* or, observing some exceptions, that *some A's are B's;* and so on.

Statistics and probability theory are attempts to *quantify the expectation* that future *A*'s will be *B*'s—in ways analogous to deductive logic's codification of the whole range of deductive inference. In sum, deduction pertains to the *necessary* relations among statements, and induction to the *contingent* relations, on the bases of which two different but complementary systems of inference are built. Together, they are far more powerful than either alone.

THE BASES OF DEDUCTION AND INDUCTION

In ordinary life, as in science, we use deduction and induction alternately to explain and to predict events, to infer the consequences of opinions and hypotheses held, to predict one phenomenon from another, and so on. One does not have to go to science to find examples. For instance, seeing a certain expression on the boss's face, Susan infers that the boss is in one of his "moods."

From what does Susan make that inference? From past experience; from past observations that when the boss screws on that expression, he is in one of his moods. In other words, Susan induced a *hypothesis* about the covariance of her boss's facial expressions and his moods. On the basis of that hypothesis, she may go further to predict certain behavior; that is, to formulate additional hypotheses amounting to a crude theory of her boss's personality. Not only are her predictions testable in the sense that the boss's behavior one way or the other is observable, but how in fact he behaves will lead to further elaborations of the "theory." And so on in common sense or science.

Because induction is essentially generalization, invariably it must go beyond the information given to make assertions (predictions) about yet unobserved future cases. The accuracy or inaccuracy of the predictions is what enables us to assign degrees of *probability* to those predictions. The risks, in science anyway, are measurable; less so in ordinary experience. An overstretched induction in common sense is called a hasty generalization, an all too commonplace fallacy that lies at the root of most prejudices and superstitions.

When reasoning inductively, care should be taken that the sample is large enough, broadly representative of the available evidence, and not selected or "edited" according to preconception. Counterexamples are ignored to one's peril where the aim is objective knowledge of the way things are (as contrasted with the way one prefers them to be).

It's a never-ending battle between controlled prediction and observation on the one hand, and wishful thinking on the other. But the fact that we *must* make inferences and projections, based on limited experience and observation, is a fact of life and survival. Whether we learn to do it well is a matter of effort and education.

It is also a matter of culture; for in the course of learning language and, later, any special techniques of inquiry and analysis, we get committed to certain underlying assumptions. In deductive reasoning, we exhibit a confidence in the *consistency* of our thought while ferreting out the inconsistencies.

The idea is that since inconsistent thinking cancels itself

out (*A and not A*), consistent thinking stands a better chance of leading not only to a valid but to a true conclusion (again, if the premises are true). In inductive reasoning, we not only invoke consistency (we want our hypotheses and explanations to be coherent), *we impose regularity and orderliness on natural phenomena.*

We see this, for instance, in assumptions about "economically rational behavior" in economics, or in trend analyses of the stock market. We assume that the recurrent happenings we observe are not mere caprice or coincidental or causally disconnected from other happenings, even where their causes are unknown. Rather, we use those regularities as clues in the search for causes.

The story of the relations between deduction and induction gets complicated in the search for causes, but the essential point is this: The *presumption* that the ways of nature are lawful and regular can never itself be proved deductively or inductively. Rather, that presumption is a *precondition* of all explanation based upon reasoning and experience. Just as deduction rests upon the unprovable law of noncontradiction, so induction rests upon the companion presumption of the uniformity of nature. Together, both assumptions add up to the conceit, in Einstein's words, that "God does not play dice."

Behind all this lies the driving motive of wanting to make sense of the world—an unquenchable curiosity that can be variously satisfied. That curiosity can in turn be shaped or misshaped. Still, as often noted in these pages, competent reasoning is not the same as knowing all the rules of logic any more than effective writing is knowing all the rules of grammar (though both are a great help!). Long before learning anything about logic or grammar, we begin to acquire certain useful (and many bad) habits of reasoning simply by learning to speak and to write. In a habitual way, we implacably absorb and obey many rules of logic in the course of learning language and a host of other skills and know-how. They enable us to think critically in everyday life and to perform tasks for which we have been specially trained. The moral of this story, then, is really quite simple: The more you know about *how* you know, the better you can know *more*.

APPENDIX B

Annotated Suggestions for Further Reading on Punctuation and Grammar

Books and pamphlets on grammar and punctuation are legion. The following books and chapters reflect the authors' bias toward quick, clear guidance on what inevitably is a topic both controversial and complex.

Chicago Manual of Style, The, 13th ed. Chicago: University of Chicago Press, 1982. A standard reference and excellent source book.

Collinson, Diane, et al. *Plain English.* Milton Keynes, England: The Open University Press, 1977. England's Open University self-teaching text; contains many exercises, diagnostic tests, and clear explanations.

Corbett, Edward P.J. *The Little Rhetoric and Handbook.* Glenview, Ill.: Scott, Foresman and Company, 1982. A not so "little" but excellent (if a trifle dull) guide to all aspects of writing and one of the few that relate writing to reasoning; in large print, beautifully produced, and, therefore, easy to follow.

Fowler, H.W. *A Dictionary of Modern English Usage,* 2nd ed. Oxford: Oxford University Press, 1965. A classic reference and gold mine of historical information; not for quick use.

Gordon, Karen E. *The Well-Tempered Sentence.* New York: Ticknor & Fields, 1983. A short, humorous survey of the rules and follies of punctuation—painless.

———. *The Transitive Vampire*. New York: Times Books, 1984. Perhaps the most readable, funny introduction to grammar in print.

Hodges, John C., and Mary E. Whitten. *Harbrace College Handbook,* 8th ed. New York: Harcourt Brace Jovanovich, 1977. A standard, beautifully laid-out reference text.

Jacobi, Ernst. *Writing at Work,* part 2. Rochelle Park, N.J.: Hayden Book Company, 1976. Clear, brief presentation of the essentials; especially good on word usage.

Strunk, William, and E.B. White. *The Elements of Style,* 3rd ed. New York: Macmillan Publishing Company, 1979. Still one of the best all-around short guides available. Chapter 1 is on "The Elementary Rules of Usage."

Williams, Joseph M. *Style: Ten Lessons in Clarity and Grace*. Glenview, Ill.: Scott, Foresman and Company, 1981. Generally excellent, but especially so on the structuring of sentences, reducing "static" and "sprawl."

Words into Type, 3rd ed. Englewood Cliffs, N.J.: Prentice-Hall, 1974. Similar to *The Chicago Manual of Style* but less academic. Contains useful advice on grammar and usage, areas that *Chicago* omits.

List of References

Acknowledgments
Dewey, John. *How We Think: A Restatement of the Relation of Reflective Thinking to the Educative Process*. In *John Dewey: The Later Works, 1925–1953,* vol. 8 (1933), edited by Jo Ann Boydston. Carbondale, Ill.: Southern Illinois University Press, 1986.

Chapter 1
Elbow, Peter. *Writing with Power*. New York: Oxford University Press, 1981.
Goodman, Nelson. *Languages of Art*. Indianapolis: Hackett, 1972.
Howard, V.A. *Artistry: The Work of Artists*. Indianapolis: Hackett, 1982.
Perkins, David N. *The Mind's Best Work*. Cambridge, Mass.: Harvard University Press, 1981.
Trimble, John R. *Writing with Style*. Englewood Cliffs, N.J.: Prentice-Hall, 1975.

Chapter 2
Elbow, Peter. *Writing with Power*. New York: Oxford University Press, 1981.
Trimble, John R. *Writing with Style*. Englewood Cliffs, N.J.: Prentice-Hall, 1975.

Zinsser, William. *On Writing Well,* 2nd ed. New York: Harper and Row, 1980.

————. *Writing with a Word Processor.* New York: Harper and Row, 1983.

Chapter 3

Berry, Thomas Elliott. *The Craft of Writing.* New York: McGraw-Hill, 1974.

Elbow, Peter. *Writing with Power.* New York: Oxford University Press, 1981.

Greene, Graham. *Ways of Escape.* New York: Penguin Books, 1981.

Hirsh, E.D., Jr. *The Philosophy of Composition.* Chicago: University of Chicago Press, 1977.

Jacobi, Ernst. *Writing at Work: Do's, Don't's, and How-to's.* Rochelle Park, N.J.: Hayden, 1976.

Payne, Lucile Vaughan. *The Lively Art of Writing.* New York: Follett Publishing Company, 1965.

Trimble, John R. *Writing with Style.* Englewood Cliffs, N.J.: Prentice-Hall, 1975.

Williams, Joseph M. *Style: Ten Lessons in Clarity and Grace* Glenview, Ill.: Scott, Foresman and Company, 1981.

Chapter 4

Nickerson, Raymond. *Notes About Reasoning.* Cambridge, Mass.: Bolt, Beranek and Newman: 1982.

————, David N. Perkins, and Edward E. Smith. *The Teaching of Thinking.* Hillsdale, N.J.: Lawrence Erlbaum Associates, 1985.

Perkins, David N., R. Allen, and J. Hafner. "Difficulties in Everyday Reasoning." In *Thinking: The Expanding Frontier,* edited by W. Maxwell. Hillsdale, N.J.: Lawrence Erlbaum Associates, 1983.

Popper, Karl R. *The Logic of Scientific Discovery,* 2nd ed. New York: Harper and Row, 1968.

Chapter 6

Churchill, Winston. *The Gathering Storm.* Boston: Houghton Mifflin, 1948.

Durrell, Lawrence. *The Dark Labyrinth*. New York: Penguin Books, 1978.

Eco, Umberto. *The Name of the Rose* New York: Harcourt Brace Jovanovich, 1980.

Greene, Graham. *Ways of Escape*. New York: Penguin Books, 1981.

Orwell, George. "Politics and the English Language." In *The Collected Essays, Journalism and Letters of George Orwell,* vol. 4, edited by Sonia Orwell and Ian Angus. New York: Harcourt Brace Jovanovich, 1968.

Powell, Anthony. *The Acceptance World*. Glascow: Fontana Books, 1967.

————. *To Keep the Ball Rolling*. New York: Penguin Books, 1983.

Index

About the Authors

Vernon A. Howard is co-founder and co-director with Israel Scheffler of the Philosophy of Education Research Center at Harvard University. He received his Ph.D. in the philosophy of science from Indiana University and completed his postdoctoral studies in philosophy and education at Harvard University. Vernon Howard has taught at universities in the United States, Canada, and England and is the recipient of several major fellowships, among them three Exxon Foundation grants (with Israel Scheffler) and a John Dewey fellowship. He lives in Cambridge, Massachusetts.

James H. Barton has thirty years' experience as a writer, beginning his career at a national newspaper, moving to a national magazine, then joining a leading educational enterprise and two of its successors. He is now an author, editorial consultant, and associate of the Philosophy of Education Research Center, contributing regularly to its Research Seminar. He holds a B.A. from Harvard University in history and literature, and an M.A. from Columbia University in comparative literature. He lives with his family in Cambridge, Massachusetts.